YOU ARE *BETTER*
THAN YOUR *BEST*

THE SECRETS TO ACHIEVING A SUCCESSFUL AND HAPPY LIFE...
IT ALL STARTS WITH YOU

LIONEL L. NOWELL III

outskirtspress
DENVER, COLORADO

Table of Contents

Acknowledgements

Undertaking any significant task requires an enormous amount of moral support, and this endeavor was no exception. Although writing this book was a labor of love, I owe a great deal of gratitude and thanks to numerous people who were instrumental in helping me turn my dreams into reality.

In particular I want to say a special thank you to my mother, Delores, and my dear departed father, Lionel Jr. Your love, guidance, and prayers were the foundation for the success and happiness that I enjoy today.

To my children, Tiffany, Michelle, Justin, and Jared, thank you for your unrelenting motivation, support, and encouragement to write this book. And, for my grandchildren Grant, Olivia, Gabe, Sean, and Aaron, I hope some day you will read this book and it will propel you to be better than your best.

To my family and friends, the personal relationships that I share with each and every one of you have been instrumental in helping me become a better person, and accomplish meaningful things in my life. I hope this book will serve as an inspiration to encourage you to always chase your dreams.

John Horan, I truly appreciated your guidance, suggestions, and perspective. Matt and Nancy McKenna, David Rickard, Larry Thompson, Joe and Winnie Davis, and others too innumerable to mention, your friendship, wise counsel, insights, and mentorship have been invaluable to me over the years.

To my colleagues at PepsiCo, Pillsbury, American Electric Power, Reynolds American, South High School, The Ohio State University, and The Executive Leadership, thank you for the positive roles you have played in my personal and professional progression.

And, last but most important, I want to acknowledge Denise, my wife, best friend, and partner over the past twenty-five years. You are my heart and soul, and in good times and bad, have always been there for me. This book is our story and would not have been possible without you.

I love and sincerely appreciate all of you.

Prologue

Things you wish someone had told you…

"That which does not kill us makes us stronger" is a famous phrase from German philosopher Friedrich Nietzsche. While many scholars have exhaustively debated the merit of this particular passage, I can personally attest that when it comes to being successful and having hapiness in your life, if you lack the wisdom and knowledge required to be better than your best, it does not make you stronger, and in reality can cause you to not achieve your dreams and aspirations.

I want to be clear and straightforward from the outset. This book is not intended for everyone. It is dedicated to inspired, ambitious people who want to comprehend the secrets of success, reinvigorate oneself, take control of their destiny, and be better than their best.

At the same time, the information enunciated on the following pages will serve as a motivational guide that explicitly details the course of action young adults, business professionals, athletes, entrepreneurs, or, for that matter, any enterprising person must adhere to as they pursue success and happiness.

Along with being a comprehensive, easily understood template for enhancing your chances of achieving success, this book provides an elaborate framework for developing, and refining, the characteristics required to excel in every nuance of your life.

Considering that a vast majority of people learn and retain information when you associate it with something they can easily establish or demonstrate a connection with, in this book I provide anecdotes, stories, and tales to help you grasp the significance of what is being discussed.

In addition, I share practical examples of people from various economic, educational, and social backgrounds that have put into effect the necessary sequence of events required to obtain the absolute best out of everything they encounter.

I elaborate on the traits required to be both successful and happy because I truly believe they are intertwined. You cannot have true success without coupling it with a happy life. And, the fact of the matter is you do not pursue success and happiness, you create it.

Invariably on almost a daily basis I encounter someone — a college student, person in an entry-level position, mid-level manager, senior executive, entrepreneur, unemployed person, stay-at-home mom/dad, you name it — all of whom are befuddled, and quite frankly frustrated, by what they have, and have not, accomplished in their personal and/or professional lives.

While many books have been written, and numerous writers have expounded on the merits of self-help, I believe I am uniquely qualified to write this particular book. Among other things, like many of you I have faced adversity, I know how it feels to be languishing in life, unsure of which way to turn, what to do, or who to go to for support. I understand what desiring more than you have today feels like. And, I have experienced having dreams and aspirations that were bigger than what other people thought would be possible, or appropriate, for me.

But, through it all, not only did I survive, I thrived, by implementing the fundamental techniques that are thoroughly outlined in this book.

As I was growing up in my low-income, blue-collar family, being successful, financially or otherwise, was not something that we often spoke about. However, I did learn from my parents the value that comes from having determination and dedication. At an early age, my mother and father encouraged my siblings and me to always "do your best." While I never questioned that statement, I must confess, at that particular stage in my life, I was not quite sure what "do your best" actually meant.

Nevertheless, whether it was related to how I performed at school or in an athletic event, one of my parents would inevitably ask, "Did you do your best?" Provided I answered "yes," my mother or father would give me a reassuring smile, and that was customarily the end of the conversation. Therefore, I quickly learned to reply in the affirmative whenever I was confronted with the question of whether I had done my best.

Fast-forward approximately thirty years. As a dutiful parent I was having a conversation with my teenage son about the virtues of working hard on his summer job, and heartened him to always "do your best." I immediately knew my mother and father's parenting style had not been passed down to me because, unlike me at his age, without skipping a beat my son replied, "What exactly does 'do your best' mean?" I paused for a few moments and reflected back on my own life. Then, somewhat reminiscently, I meticulously began to explain to my son various perspectives on what "doing your best" meant.

At this point I should elucidate that when this particular conversation took place I had spent almost twenty years working in corporate America, participated in the negotiation of multi-billion-dollar transactions, traveled the world, ascended to senior executive status at PepsiCo, Inc., and served on several public companies' boards of directors.

And, during my career progression, I was fortunate enough to have been mentored by some of the brightest and most successful executives in the business community. In turn, I have mentored hundreds of people who have gone on to have very rewarding lives. As a result, when I was speaking with my son I felt fairly confident that I knew a thing or two about doing your best, being successful, and achieving a happy fulfilled life.

After numerous in-depth conversations, during which I proudly explained assorted scenarios to my son about excelling in what you do and being rewarded for your results, not just for your efforts, he said to me, "What you told me makes a lot of sense, but if you know so much why haven't you written a book and shared your insights with other people?"

I was initially astounded by my son's comment, but at the same time, in an aberrant way, honored and appreciative that he perceived value from what I had shared with him. In hindsight I realized that my son's inquisitiveness pertaining to why I had not written a book was a sincere, astute observation. As is the case with most ambitious people, I have attended numerous seminars and read countless books on leadership, management styles, motivating others and building teams. And over the course of my life I have been quoted in various magazines and business articles, and even contributed stories to a few books. However, prior to that specific point in time, I had not given much consideration to sharing, via my own book, what I, and other successful people I know, learned the hard way, or were taught as we progressed in our lives.

Therefore, with some trepidation I arduously accepted the challenge my son placed before me. Within this book I render a personal and unique perspective on how you should envision your life, and obtain the success and happiness you desire. What you will acquire in each of the chapters is a practical, down-to-earth, real-life approach to being a better you.

Through writing "You Are Better Than Your Best," my goal is to share with others the wisdom a myriad of people have so graciously imparted to me over the past thirty-plus years. As a result, I have devoted a significant amount of time, energy, and extraordinary effort to ensure readers will derive some valuable knowledge and insights. In the process I did not engage any topic included in this book frivolously, and truly believe the contents will be beneficial to anyone who studiously applies what is articulated throughout the various chapters.

Looking back on everything that has manifested itself in my life, I am living proof that if you activate the three D's — Desire, Determination, and Dedication — dreams do come true. A successful, happy, and meaningful life is attainable by anyone who commits to putting a thoughtful plan in place ("Desire"), is devoted to doing whatever it takes to achieve what is depicted in their plan ("Determination"), and continuously strives to be better than their best ("Dedication").

Regardless of your current occupation, personal status, financial situation, or the circumstances you are facing, I am convinced that after reading this book you will possess the knowledge, perceptiveness, and motivation required to accomplish your dreams and live a more meaningful life. It all starts with you.

Booker T. Washington, who was a prominent American figure and an accomplished educator, author, and political leader, was quoted as saying; "Success in life is founded upon attention to the small things rather than to the large things; to the everyday thing nearest to us rather than to the things that are remote and uncommon."

While I may not know you personally, I believe there is a divine plan for you to prosper, and deep within yourself you process the three D's — Desire, Determination, and Dedication — required to achieve a successful and happy life. Everything that you want to accomplish in your life is possible. You just need the confidence, guidance, and support, which you will derive from reading this book, to turn your dreams into reality.

I have the utmost faith in you and your abilities. Now it is up to you to determine the path that will change your future. Start by believing in yourself and "Stop Being an Underachiever," because you are about to discover that "You Are Better Than Your Best."

Lionel L. Nowell III

CHAPTER One

Stop Being an Underachiever

Believing you can and will be successful is much more impactful than focusing on all of the reasons why you cannot…

Have you ever wondered why some individuals flourish in their chosen profession, achieve tremendous success in life, and are happy, while other people put forth great effort and still fail to maximize their talents, or reach their full potential? Is it luck, influence, fate, or are these high achievers just more astute than the rest of us? While all of the aforementioned attributes may play a role, I believe there are other qualities that are more telling when it comes to prognosticating success.

In the course of conducting research for this book, I encountered a number of bright, energetic, talented individuals who were bewildered in their quest to navigate the maze life had set before them. These were intelligent men and women who attended some of the top universities and graduate schools in the world, and they were identified as high potential, and future leaders, by their respective organizations. Yet, when it came to their professional careers and personal lives, they underachieved.

The question of why some people attain success and happiness while others seem to falter, and never reach their full potential, is perplexing. And, while I do not profess to have all of the answers, based on my personal experiences and observing people, some of whom succeeded and others who failed, I discovered there are some fundamental attributes that influence the end results. Therefore, throughout this book I am going to share with you some secrets of success that it took me years to learn.

When I was growing up my father and mother instilled into me the value of hard work, treating other people with respect, having high integrity, and always doing my best. While I learned later in life that it would take more than just those characteristics to achieve all of my dreams and aspirations, I am proud to say the core values my parents instilled in me have been the foundation for most of my notable accomplishments.

Both of my parents were blessed with good common sense, but the truth is that neither one of them was college educated; in fact, they did not even graduate from high school. However, limited formal education, and not possessing a high-school diploma, did not prevent my parents from having immense expectations for their children.

While we were not well off financially, my mother and father saw to it that what we lacked in money was more than compensated for through their love, support, and spiritual guidance.

When I was in junior high school I vividly remember accompanying my father as he went about his second job of cleaning office buildings at night. One evening I snuck away to one of the executive offices and jumped into the big overstuffed leather desk chair. Swirling around in that chair, I dreamed of having a spacious office resembling the one I was in, and wondered what it would be like to be a successful business executive. Somewhere in the midst of my getting lost in this dream, my father came up behind me and put his large hands on my shoulders. I will never forget that moment when he said, "It can be more gratifying to make a living using your brains instead of your hands, and if you study hard and get a great education, this could be your office one day."

I am sure I did not realize it at that particular moment, but my father's words have stuck with me over the years, and he inspired me to never give up on my dreams.

Providing for five kids was an enormous task for my parents, and needless to say stashing money away for college was not in the family budget. So by working miscellaneous part-time jobs after school, and sometimes two jobs during the summer months, I scraped and saved every penny I could muster. And, through perseverance, diligence, and unwavering support from family members, friends, and teachers/professors, I graduated from South High School, in Columbus, Ohio, and was the first of my siblings to attend and graduate from college, The Ohio State University.

Not unlike many of my fellow college classmates, I entered the "real" world excited about the opportunities that lay ahead yet filled with anxiety at the same time. I was primed for success, but in actuality I was naïve about what it would take to achieve it.

While most universities do a tremendous job of providing students the prerequisite technical and theoretical skills, they are not as adept when it comes to educating students in the fundamental soft skills, which are essential to procuring a meaningful and successful life. Therefore, a majority of students graduate from college never having learned, or been introduced to, the attributes necessary to be better than your best.

As a college student I operated in a regimented, structured environment, which required a limited amount of independent decision-making. Upon graduation I entered a demanding, complex world and began a journey that was completely unstructured. Although I was armed with a college degree, I was not remotely prepared for the challenges and obstacles that would be situated in my path.

- The reality is that when I graduated from college I was scared, perplexed, and conflicted with more questions than answers.

- Who could I trust and talk openly and honest with when I need career counseling, have an issue with a boss, or want advice on how to manage my finances?

- How should I go about managing personal and professional relationships, and fostering the right business contacts?

- Should I take a job or career opportunity I do not like, and am not interested in, just for the money?

- Do I admit it when I do not understand something, or is that an admission of not being qualified or smart enough?

- Who would be a good mentor or sponsor, and how do I go about getting one?

It was almost as if I had spent the first twenty-two years of my life in a protective bubble, and now for the first time my future success, or failure, was all on my shoulders.

I recite this story because like most of the people reading this book I have experienced and understand the dilemma of wanting to do well, but not being quite sure how to go about attaining success.

The exhilarating thing I discovered is that although your background, family circumstances, previous failures, past relationships, and everything you have gone through up to this point in your life might have influenced the person you are today, ultimately you are responsible for making the changes that determine who you will become tomorrow.

As for me, despite confronting what many people would probably consider insurmountable odds, I redefined myself and acclimated to new situations and environments. Along the way I experienced numerous ups and downs, and made my fair share of mistakes and blunders; but ultimately I prevailed.

Through the process of my own personal experiences, coupled with watching what did and did not work for many of my friends and colleagues, I accumulated a significant amount of insight into what it takes to live a happy, fulfilled life.

This led me to the conclusion that most people do not underachieve, and fail to maximize their full potential, because they are not smart, or due to lack of hard work or effort on their part. The primary reason individuals achieve less than they are capable of is a result of their not believing in themselves and having the confidence to forge ahead when others suggest it is better to quit and give up.

As the famous inventor Thomas Edison once said, "If we did the things we are capable of, we would astound ourselves."

While some people may think it is a cliché that so many self-help and motivational books stress the importance of focusing on positive experiences and not dwelling on negative past experiences, I cannot emphasize enough the power of this advice. However, I am also very aware of the fact that most successful people endured multiple setbacks on their path to success. Therefore, in this book I divulge some nuggets of wisdom related to perseverance and inner strength that I wish someone had extended to me early in my life.

I also share insights from senior executives, athletes, religious leaders, and normal people like you and me, who have encountered, and successfully navigated, the obstacles most of us face on a daily basis.

Many of you have undoubtedly been told, at one time or another, by a teacher, family member, boss, or so-called friend, what they believe you can, and cannot, accomplish in your life. Succumbing to other people's opinions concerning what is best for you, or being told you cannot do something or that you are not smart enough or good enough, can result in you pursuing your dreams without a winning attitude, or worst yet culminates in you totally abandoning your dreams and aspirations. And, if you listen to and follow the misguided advice of people who have a demarcated view of your future, their adverse perspective will breed negativity in you and cause you to be an underachiever.

Therefore, one of the first lessons you need to learn is that you cannot let opposing or hostile people play a debilitating role in your life. Success cannot be achieved if doubt or apprehension is given any access into the shaping of your dreams.

Learning to be self-motivated, and making a monumental change in your life, starts with "you" the man — or woman as it may be — that is staring back at you when you look in the mirror.

While being afraid is a natural feeling that you sometimes experience, being reluctant or unwilling to pursue your dreams because you lack self-confidence can be paralyzing. So, along with making positive, proactive changes in your life, you also must be diligent and refute anyone or anything that is attempting to confine your dreams or prevent you from reaching your destiny.

History is rampant with illustrations of people who, when told they could not do something, used that negativity to fuel their motivation and prove the naysayers wrong.

Visualize in your mind a five-year-old boy who stutters. The first day of school, due to his stuttering, his schoolmates laugh at him, and he is so embarrassed that for the next eight years he pretends to be mute, refusing to speak aloud in school, and communicates only by writing. This continues throughout his childhood until a teacher takes an interest and encourages him to read a poem he has written in front of the entire class. While he is obviously nervous, the boy, who has now grown into a young man, commits the poem's verses to memory and discovers that by doing so he can speak without stuttering.

The teacher goes on to encourage him to recite a poem in class each day. This leads to him competing in high-school debates and oratorical contests, and during his senior year of high school the young man wins a public-speaking contest. He goes on to pursue acting studies and ends up becoming a famous theater and film actor.

This is not a made-up tale. It is the story of "James Earl Jones," who is well known for his deep bass voice. Perhaps you know him best as the voice of *Star Wars'* Darth Vader, or as Mufasa in *The Lion King*.

James Earl Jones, the man who stuttered as a child and was ridiculed by his fellow students, admitted at one point that he still thinks about what he says carefully before saying it, but despite all he endured Jones did not let others define him.

Some people did not think James Earl Jones would ever speak without stuttering, yet he has gone on to perform in over fifty films, as well as have memorable roles onstage and in television. In the process he won numerous honors, including three Emmys and two Tony Awards.

This is just one of the many examples of individuals who went on to accomplish great things in their lives because they had a conviction in themselves and did not let preconceptions dictate for them what was possible.

Each of the subsequent chapters of this book will reveal actionable strategies you can utilize to assist you in discovering how to "Stop Being an Underachiever." Additionally, I will share some simplistic yet effective techniques that can enable you to get what you want out of life.

Although there are certainly times when it makes perfect sense to be a leader and not a follower, I still contend that one of the best ways to establish winning habits is to emulate winners. And one of the most important attributes of successful people, no matter how you choose to define success, is their ability to be flexible and open to new ideas and unique circumstances. The world is fluid and constantly changing, so you have to embrace the new opportunities that are placed in your path and be adaptable to achieve success.

As this book will iterate, in order to accomplish your goals it is imperative that you adhere to the three D's — Desire, Determination, and Dedication. With a thoughtful plan (Desire), meticulous execution (Determination), and a passion for excellence (Dedication), you will accomplish great things in your life.

Along with implementing the three D's, you must also be cognizant of the fact that you cannot saunter around and wait for facts, circumstances, or states of affairs to happen for you, or to you. To "Stop Being an Underachiever" requires that you quit procrastinating, develop a sense of urgency, step out of your comfort zone, assume control of your own destiny, conquer the obstacles that are hindering your prosperity, and initiate the changes you want to see in your life.

At the beginning of this introductory chapter, I wrote that "believing you can, and will, be successful is much more impactful than focusing on all the reasons you cannot."

A news report that embodies this message is the signing of the Northern Ireland peace accord, which is known universally as "The Good Friday Agreement." This agreement ended decades of horrible violence and bloodshed in the six counties of Northern Ireland, bringing all parties to a miraculous accord, which culminated in the end of the fighting.

The United States envoy to this peace process was former United States Senator George Mitchell, who labored in earnest for two years attempting to bring the two sides together in Northern Ireland.

When interviewed after its historic signing, Senator Mitchell was noted as saying that the settlement represented seven hundred days of failure and one day of success.

I have always found Senator Mitchell's statement to be the perfect formula for success. First, the days of failure were numerous and exhausting, but Senator Mitchell and his staff never once let that dash their hope or affect their performance for the next day. They firmly believed their perseverance could be vital in helping to formulate a peaceful resolution to the violence and bloodshed, and they never gave up despite those recurring days of failure.

Second, Senator Mitchell's statement also is impactful in that it stresses the ultimate success over the more than seven hundred days of failure. Senator Mitchell put the extended process into perspective but in no way dwelled on it. I believe he invoked the seven hundred days of failure to reflect how persistence can lead to success. And, in the end a significant success will always erase any negative vibes of the setbacks that preceded it along the way.

It does not matter if you are negotiating a peace treaty, interviewing for a job, starting a new venture, or repairing a splintered relationship - you cannot let temporary adversity allow you to lose focus on your ultimate objective.

Throughout this book I am going to rebuke some myths and unveil some truths, which will facilitate your adopting a positive attitude, thereby enabling you to achieve new heights and enjoy even greater accomplishments.

Along with having an indisputable belief in yourself, it is never too early to start thinking positive thoughts and pursuing advantageous actions, which will propel you toward your ultimate goal. The fact is, successful people possess a winner's mentality and expect to win. On the surface that sounds pretty fundamental, doesn't everyone want to win? However, when you delve a little deeper it becomes apparent that even more important than wanting to win, successful people hate to lose.

Until you reach a point in your life where you hate to lose, you will continue to underachieve and not make the necessary changes required to yield sustainable success and happiness.

Your commitment to success must be tenacious because you are the only person who can prevent you from attaining what you want to accomplish in your life.

Automotive and assembly line industrialist Henry Ford was quoted as saying, "Whether you think you can or think you can't, you're right." In other words, if you think you can't do something it will prevent you from succeeding. However, if you think you can, it will drive you to success and happiness.

Many self-help experts express that one of the secrets to success is mastering how to be a team player. While I cannot disagree with this assessment, I can attest that if you do not have individual skills and bring value to the team, you will not be on the team. Consequently, you will not find the true success and happiness you are pursuing by totally relying on other people, or other factors that are beyond your control. To reach your goals you have to stay focused on the things that are in your control, and maintain steadfast faith and unwavering belief in yourself.

Trust me, there is no magic formula to being successful, and no one can do for you what you are unwilling to do for yourself. You have to strive for excellence each and every day, and not be reluctant to take prudent risks, endure mistakes, or implement the necessary changes required for you to be better than your best. At the same time you need to be inquisitive, and challenge yourself to continuously learn new things that allow you to take advantage of opportunities other people miss, or simply see as not worth the effort.

Ultimately you have to become comfortable with who you are, and acknowledge that while life is not easy, and things do not always go your way, you will accomplish transcendental feats regardless of the obstacles placed in your path.

You are a winner, and I truly believe you have the desire, determination, and dedication required to be successful. So "Stop Being an Underachiever" and get prepared for a fantastic journey that is going to enrich your life, because "You Are Better Than Your Best."

CHAPTER TWO

You Are Better Than Your Best

You either get better or you get worse; no one stays the same…

Desire, determination, and dedication are necessary traits to possess, and when utilized appropriately they will definitely augment the chances of you reaching your goals. However, what you accomplish, how prosperous you are, and what impact you forge will also be dictated by your ability to effectively navigate the various challenges and opportunities you undoubtedly will encounter on a day-to-day basis.

Most people go through life just trying to fit in. Their preference is to go along with the status quo and not push the boundaries. In fact, blending in with the crowd and not standing out can seem natural, because it makes you feel comfortable and removes the pressure of your having to compete and eradicate barriers.

Think about it. As you were growing up, how many times were you told by your parents, a teacher, or perhaps even a coach, before you were about to engage in something that you were unsure of or did not want to participate in, "Just do your best"? And when you were asked how well you had done you unequivocally responded, "I did my best."

The truth is, most of you are not even certain what "doing your best" really comprises. As a result you behave in a manner that seems normal, or is appealing, to those around you, and are content to remain in your comfort zone.

Sadly, if you become satisfied with your current situation, and where you are in life, you will never actualize your full potential or become the best you can be.

To be successful in any aspect of your life, you cannot become complacent and accept being average. You have to put everything on the line, get out of your comfort zone, and eliminate the just-do-your-best attitude. Quite frankly, just doing enough is not good enough.

I was watching a documentary related to the great white shark and discovered an amazing revelation. This particular breed of shark must maintain a constant forward swimming motion to breathe, or else they will die.

Although the television program was referencing the anatomy of sharks, I could not help but think about how the same analogy could be applied to any aspect of our lives. To be successful you can never, even for one minute, become totally satisfied with what you have accomplished, and be unwilling to move forward and abandon your comfort zone in the process. You have to constantly strive to keep moving and doing more. Otherwise you risk becoming a dead shark.

I understand that for many people making a behavioral change, and eradicating the just-do-your-best attitude, are among the most difficult things to do, because we have grown up in a society where fitting in, or just doing as well as the next person, is perceived as being good enough.

Let me share with you a couple of examples related to what I am referring. In a number of youth sports leagues every person, on every team, receives a trophy, whether their team wins or loses. Why? Because we want to make everyone feel equal, by not distinguishing the people who perform well from those who do not. Furthermore, many educational institutions do not believe students should be competing for grades and striving to excel. As a result these institutions have completely abolished grades altogether, and moved to a simple pass/fail model. Hence, as long as you achieve average results, and do as well as most of the other people in the class, you are considered to have done okay.

Merely trying to blend in with the crowd is a guaranteed recipe for how not to be better than your best. You were born to stand out, not blend in. To be successful in your life you have to break away from the masses, make a meaningful difference, and not be averse to traveling an uncharted path. You cannot expect other people to subsidize you, and you cannot settle for, or become satisfied with, accomplishing anything less than what you are truly capable of.

In the *real* world there are absolute winners and losers. You are rewarded for your results, not for your efforts, and success is not achieved by being mediocre in your endeavors.

To ensure there is no misunderstanding or confusion with what I am saying, let me be perfectly clear. While the absolute winners and losers in the world can be distinguished by their desire, determination, and dedication, you also have to appreciate that failure in a single endeavor is not fatal, and in no way signifies that a person is a loser. Some of the best knowledge comes from negative experiences. Therefore, sometimes you just need to stay fixated on the goals you are pursuing and remain determined and dedicated to improving; these two components are essential to your success.

Early in my professional career, the company's chief financial officer assigned me to a new product introduction project. This task was extremely important to me because it was the first undertaking where I was working primarily on my own, and it required a significant amount of financial analysis.

When I finished the assignment and wrote up my conclusions, I proudly took the completed project to my manager for her review. Without even glancing at what I had presented to her she asked, "Is this your best work?"

I was momentarily speechless and not quite sure how to answer the question. If I said, "Yes, this is my best work," and it was not up to the meticulous standard that she expected, I would have just confirmed to her I was not capable of delivering a high-quality output. On the other hand if I said, "No this is not my best work," then she could rightly question why I would bring her something that was not comprehensive and complete. After a few seconds that seemed like hours, I said, "I worked extremely hard on this project but I would be interested in your assessment."

Without hesitation she declared, "I know this analysis will be good, and you put forth what you consider to be your best effort, but with a little more time and extra focus I am sure it could be improved upon, because 'You Are Better Than Your Best.'"

Needless to say I was shocked and devastated by my manager's comments. How could she suggest I could do better without even looking at what I had prepared?

Feeling a little exasperated I trudged back to my desk and asked a colleague to read over the final report. To my surprise he found a couple of errors, not major ones but nonetheless they were there. My colleague also asked me a few probing questions that caused me to rethink and expand on the conclusions I had reached.

At that moment I began to understand that what my manager had told me was completely accurate. I could in fact do better than what I'd envisioned was my best.

The reality is that no matter how superlative something may appear to be, with the proper amount of additional focus, and extra effort, it can always be improved upon. Just approaching or looking at a situation with a different attitude, and expanding the puissance you put forth, can make it exceedingly better.

To derive outstanding results in any facet of your life, you must acknowledge the necessity of having intense focus and putting forth extraordinary effort.

Being an avid basketball fan, I always enjoyed watching Michael Jordan play. Jordan is a Naismith Memorial Hall of Fame inductee, and many consider him the greatest basketball player of all time. Personally, for me, Michael Jordan defined what being a winner meant.

Michael Jordan retired from basketball during his prime to pursue a career in baseball, and a year later returned to basketball. Despite the disdain from some critics who, upon Jordan's return to basketball, insisted that he was too old to make an impact and was even "washed up," Jordan proceeded to lead the Chicago Bulls to three consecutive National Basketball Association championships.

I admire Michael Jordan because he had an unrelenting desire to be successful, and this fueled his determination and dedication to be better than his best. Jordan also did not allow other people to define for him what he could or could not accomplish, and his remarkable story emphasizes that you must always believe in yourself and not succumb to what other people are saying about you.

Many people have the natural ability and talent to do great things in their area of pursuit, yet compelling natural abilities mean absolutely nothing if desire, determination, and dedication are discarded.

Therefore, no matter what personal or professional goal you are pursuing, you have to constantly challenge yourself to go beyond what you, and others, think is reasonable or acceptable.

Here are a few simple yet salient action steps you can adopt to assist you in being better than your best.

Action steps for being better than your best:

- Always, and I do mean always, give 100% effort. Expect to win, and do whatever it takes to ensure you provide yourself the best possible opportunity to succeed.

- Look, act, and speak with confidence. If you do not believe in yourself no one else will either.

- Spend ample time upfront obtaining clarity on the expectations and timing, and then exceed those expectations. Also, do not be hesitant to ask questions, or admit when you are not clear on something.

- Listen and think before you speak or act. Taking the time to analyze what is being said, and/or review the information being presented to you, will provide you the opportunity to reflect and make the appropriate strategic responses.

- Be proactive and commence working on whatever it is you are trying to accomplish sooner rather than later. All of us to an extent procrastinate, but learning to use your time wisely can be a huge advantage in determining your ultimate success.

- Do extensive research. Be detailed and know the subject matter inside and out. Investing the time upfront to investigate and learn will be extremely beneficial in the long run.

- Challenge the status quo, but support your findings with facts, not emotions. Everything can be improved upon with the proper amount of time and extra effort. The key is approaching the situation with the right attitude.

- Leverage all of your resources, internal and external, to assist you in whatever endeavor you pursue. Do not be reluctant to ask for help, advice, or counsel when it is required to enhance the ultimate outcome.

- Be unconditionally committed. Devote the time, and effort, that is required to dramatically improve upon whatever it is you are working on.

- Check and double-check your assumptions, facts, and figures.

- Anticipate, and have answers for questions that might be posed. Be proactive and prepared, as opposed to being reactive and resistant.

- Know the intended audience. Who are you trying to impress, influence, or convince? Design the final report or presentation to meet their style and preference.

- Maintain conviction in your final analysis, but also be flexible and open-minded when drawing conclusions or making recommendations.

- Involve a *trusted* colleague in the review and critique of your work. Utilizing someone you have confidence in to assist you in analyzing where, and how, you can embellish your ideas is an advantage that should not be underestimated.

- When you believe you have done your absolute best, give it one more final review seeking ways to improve and make it even better.

With a well-thought-out plan (desire), continuous effort (determination), and the appropriate attitude (dedication), there are no limitations to how well you can do, how far you can go, or how successful you can be. Furthermore, you should never settle for being average, and definitely not let other people define for you what your best is.

In conversing with people I respect, I have come to comprehend that successful people take challenges head on. In fact, sometimes they create challenges where they did not exist, because only by pushing yourself will you truly determine what your best is.

By the same token, I do not know of anyone who has succeeded in everything they have attempted to do. The truth is, most people fail multiple times before ultimately succeeding. To be better than your best it is imperative that you take prudent risks, and you cannot be afraid to fail. If by chance you do happen to fail you have to try again, if you fail a second time, you have to make a few adjustments and try again, if you fail the third time, make a few more adjustments and try yet again.

If you stop, or quit, pursuing your goals and objectives, the result is permanent; however, if you keep going, you retain the ability to change the outcome. Persistence will always overcome failure, and a temporary heartache, or setback, is just a setup for greater success.

Even when you have accomplished a worthwhile goal you should be happy with what you have achieved, but not become too satisfied, because you can always do better.

A colleague told me that some years ago he accompanied a friend to a Korean martial-arts school to observe the training regimen. On the wall in the lounge area was a posting, of which he later asked the hapkido master if he could quickly borrow to copy.

The placard contained a list with the heading "Portrait of an Achiever," and the following items were listed below:

- Failed in Business - Bankruptcy, 1831

- Defeated for Legislature, 1832

- Failed in Business - Bankruptcy, 1834

- Sweetheart - Fiancée Dies, 1835

- Nervous Breakdown, 1836

- Defeated in Election, 1838

- Defeated for U.S. Congress, 1843

- Defeated Again for U.S. Congress, 1846

- Defeated Once Again for U.S. Congress, 1848

- Defeated for U.S. Senate, 1855

- Defeated for U.S. Vice President, 1856

- Defeated Again for U.S. Senate, 1858

- Elected President of the U.S., 1860

     "Abraham Lincoln"

"You cannot fail unless you quit."

This remarkable list of setbacks by the great President Abraham Lincoln highlights the challenges he encountered on his way to success. Although Lincoln endured numerous obstacles in his life that could have resulted in him quitting, and giving up, he did not let other people, or difficult circumstances, define for him who he would ultimately become. Despite what some would have perceived as failures,

Abraham Lincoln was ultimately successful because he had a plan for his life (desire), constantly focused on putting forth extraordinary effort (determination), and maintained a positive attitude (dedication), the three things that distinguish a winner from a loser.

Oddly enough, when my colleague's friend received his black belt in martial arts, he was told that the Korean word for black belt is "Cho Dan." When he asked what "Cho Dan" meant in Korean, it was explained to him that it meant "beginner."

When someone reaches the coveted first-degree black belt rank he or she cannot become complacent and stop putting forth the desire, determination, and dedication that got him or her to where they are today. They have to continue training as diligently as they did when they were a beginner. And, he or she must constantly concentrate on their determination and dedication in training so that they can improve even more.

I quizzed a number of the successful people I spoke with while writing this book about how they achieved their personal success. One of the primary things almost all of them stressed they do is have big dreams, coupled with a high expectation that those dreams will be achieved. Their counsel was to "dream big, but execute your dreams as if your life depends on it."

A person I deeply admire, and someone whom I consider a very good friend, is Dr. Kathryn D. Sullivan. The first American woman to walk in space and see earth from a totally different perspective, Dr. Sullivan is a veteran of three space shuttle missions and a 2004 inductee into the Astronaut Hall of Fame.

When asked what qualities are important in becoming a first-class astronaut Dr. Sullivan replied, "You need an interesting mix of vision and optimism with realism and skepticism: the first two let you dream and reach; the last two help you actually turn the dream into some reality."

Many people go through life hoping the right things will happen for them or to them, as opposed to taking personal responsibility and making things happen. Successful people seize control of their destiny and understand the importance of having defined goals and objectives. By failing to plan you are subconsciously planning to fail, and hope is not a strategy.

If you do not possess defined goals for your life you lack vision, and without a vision you do not have options, and without options you have a limited chance for success.

I once heard a story about former Congressman Jack Kemp, who prior to entering politics was a professional football quarterback for 13 years.

During Kemp's senior year of college, the football coach purportedly called him into his office and told the young Kemp that of all the people on the team, he thought Kemp was the only one who could make it to the professional football league. The coach inspired Kemp and made him believe that if he worked harder he could become a professional football player.

Many years later, Kemp spoke at a dinner where many of his former college teammates were in attendance. He gave a speech about his career and how that single meeting with his college coach helped motivate him to exert the strenuous effort required to practice and play like a professional. Following the speech, Kemp was shocked when each of his teammates relayed to him how the coach had brought each one of them into his office and given the same speech — that if they worked hard enough and sacrificed enough, they were the only one on their college team that could become a professional football player.

The story goes that Kemp was furious — for about a minute. Then as he thought about it, he realized that the coach had provided him, and each of his teammates, with a vision for the future, which motivated every one of them to strive harder to achieve their full potential.

The fact of the matter is that as a college senior Jack Kemp received a lesson in life on desire, determination, and dedication.

This story only conveys in a stronger and more compelling way that exceptional achievement is not something that comes to you randomly. Each and every day you have to consciously proceed toward your goals, even if it is only in a small way.

Imagine for a moment your life as a journey. If you begin any journey without defined goals or objectives, there is no assurance where you will end up. But, just having dreams and goals does not guarantee success. I have known a number of people who had big dreams, and undoubtedly that is an admirable attribute. However, the fact is some of these same people never accomplished anything, and staggered through their lives aimlessly lost, without a purpose. Why? Because just having desires and big dreams is not enough. You need to have determination and dedication, and activate a plan to achieve your goals and objectives.

Now to be perfectly blunt, I also am not suggesting that merely having stated goals and objectives, and putting a plan in motion, will result in you being better than your best. That is far from the truth. However, knowing where you are headed, how you intend to get there, and pushing yourself to do exceedingly more than what is expected of you is definitely a good starting point.

As you are pursuing your goals you also can never place your future in someone else's hands, or allow other people's decisions to dictate what you will, or will not, achieve. You are the *only* person who is completely responsible for your success or failure, and are where you are today because of the good and bad choices you have made. Therefore, as scary as it may seem, your future success and happiness, or failure and unhappiness, is entirely up to you.

Accepting responsibility for your own actions is a prerequisite to a successful and fulfilled life. When you cease blaming other people or inconsequential circumstances for your current situation, and realize that you alone are responsible for your fate, you will start to accomplish all of the great things you want to manifest in your life.

I cannot begin to recite the myriad of people I have encountered who profess to have problems with their boss, coworkers, spouse, children, friends, you name it. They readily admit to not being happy or content with their lives. Yet day after day, over and over again, they continue to engage in the same activities that are contributing to their being discontented.

Doing the same thing time after time the same way, and expecting to get different results, has been defined as insanity, but it could just as well be termed being completely irresponsible.

Rather than taking responsibility, focusing on what they can change, and making a conscientious decision to alleviate those actions, some people choose to only focus on all of the reasons they cannot change. If you want to be euphoric you have to embrace the endeavors that make you happy, and rid yourself of the situations and conditions in your life that are contributing to your being unhappy. It sounds simplistic and in a lot of ways it is just that basic.

The more responsibility you assume for what is happening in your life, the more control you will have. The more control you have the happier you will be. And the happier you are, the more success you will achieve. To be better than your best you have to be assertive and accept responsibility for every aspect of your behavior.

Your life will be punctuated with a lot of twists and turns, but you are ultimately responsible for where you end up, and what you attain along the way.

You should never think of yourself as being average, and not let anyone or anything define you, or preclude you from completing what you set out to accomplish. You are the only one who can thwart your plan for attaining what you desire.

One of the most majestic birds in the world is an eagle. An eagle soars through the sky and commands respect from all of the other creatures that inhabit the air. An eagle is also a bird of prey, which lives off of what it kills for food.

On the opposite extreme of the eagle is the chicken. A chicken is a rather meek bird that stays close to its roost, and although it can fly, it spends the majority of its life walking around on the ground. A chicken also finds its food by pecking in the dirt for seeds and insects, or eating what people decide to feed it. And in the end, someone, or something, usually feasts on the chicken.

The point is that as you evolve and live your life, you have to decide if you are going to command respect and soar like the *eagle*, or be complacent and settle for being mediocre like the *chicken*.

"You Are Better Than Your Best," so set your sights high, ascend like an eagle, expect to succeed, and along the way "Master the Rules of the Game."

CHAPTER Three

Master the Rules of the Game

Life is simple; people make it complicated…

Interpersonal skills, or what others may define as people skills, social skills, or communication skills, are often underestimated when identifying traits required for being successful. However, learning to develop, and utilize, interpersonal skills to your advantage is a talent that can be critically important in the pursuit of your success.

The House of Representatives, on charges of perjury and obstruction of justice, impeached former President William Jefferson "Bill" Clinton during his second term in office. Although the Senate subsequently acquitted him, President Clinton exited the presidency having been only the second president impeached.

Yet, when George W. Bush succeeded him as president, Clinton had the highest end-of-office approval rating of any United States president since World War II. Considering President Clinton's moral, ethical, and legal challenges, you might be a little surprised by this revelation and wonder how that could be possible.

The fact of the matter is, while public opinion of President Clinton's politics varies, Republicans, Democrats, and Independents alike would argue that one of President Clinton's greatest strengths was his interpersonal skills.

Known for being deliberate in his communication style, President Clinton made it a point to connect with people when he spoke, and always took the time to ponder, and carefully consider the questions posed to him, before he answered.

Utilizing his polished interpersonal skills, which he developed during his earlier years in public office, President Clinton was able to engage with his audience and present his views in a calm, logical, and in a majority of cases, convincing manner.

While past presidents and politicians of both major parties faded away, as a result of his oratorical skills President Clinton endured and remains a highly sought-after speaker for fundraising events, whether they are political or philanthropic. And, regardless of your political views and what you may think of him, due in part to his legendary interpersonal skills, President Clinton may well go down in history as one of the great politicians of the 20th century.

There is a lot of merit to the phrase "first impressions are lasting impressions," but ironically many people significantly undervalue the importance of communicating, networking, and building mutually beneficial relationships. In this era of texting, Twitter, e-mails, and multimedia-enabled smart phones, people have forgotten, or worst yet never learned, the meaningful benefits that are derived from personal, face-to-face interactions.

An example that stands out in my memory, and emphasizes the impact of the digital age, relates to what occurred during the 2010 World Cup. Italy is a country where soccer is preeminent, supported by the fact that they have won four World Cup championships. In 2010, as the defending champions, people in Italy were hoping for their soccer team to win yet another World Cup, thereby giving them consecutive championships.

However, soccer fans throughout the world were dismayed when the Italian squad made a shockingly early exit from the tournament.

Following their unexpected loss a bishop in Italy wrote a column in a Catholic newspaper, which expressed the notion that going forward Italy would no longer be a force in world soccer. His rationale was that in this day and age, young men in Italy spend far too much time with their Xboxes and computers, as opposed to previous generations that made playing soccer a staple of their daily routine.

The Catholic bishop theorized, and others throughout Europe agreed, that in the future champions of soccer would come from underde-veloped countries where impoverished youth do not have access to high-tech gadgets, but have plenty of access to the free activity of playing soccer.

Although the bishop's argument was in essence a pleading for the young men in Italy to enhance their interaction with soccer balls, the same basic principle could be applied to your personal interac-tion with people. If you do not focus on perfecting your interpersonal skills, you will not be prepared to win the World Cups that exist in your life.

When I graduated from college and commenced my first professional role, I undervalued the importance of interpersonal skills, and as a result was not very social at work. The truth is I did not appreciate, or believe it was necessary to, network or interact with my peers beyond what was required to accomplish my assigned responsibilities. It was not that I disliked my colleagues (okay, some of them I was not par-ticularly fond of), but the point was that I grew up being taught that when you were getting compensated to do a job, your sole purpose for being there was to work, not make friends.

Needless to say I was working hard, but did not seem to receive the same recognition, or have the same job fulfillment, that some of my fellow colleagues obtained. The fact of the matter is by denying the group dynamics, and not leveraging my interpersonal skills, I was limiting the resources I had access to.

While there may be a few people who think they can accomplish everything all by themselves, successful people realize they need to embrace the support of their family, friends, and colleagues to enhance their effectiveness.

In my case, I observed how my colleagues fostered social connections, and leveraged personal relationships, to get more accomplished. While no one openly discussed what was going on, it became apparent that personally interacting with various people throughout the organization allowed my colleagues to tap into a network of resources, as well as establish a support group, which made them more productive.

I must admit that initially I was frustrated and upset over the praise my colleagues were receiving. How could it be that I was working longer hours and more diligently than my counterparts, yet they were getting promoted, not just because of what they knew, but also because of whom they knew, and how they leveraged those relationships? After observing this phenomenon occur time and time again, I began to realize my colleagues were not slackers or underperformers; they were just being more astute at utilizing their social skills than I was.

Through mimicking my colleagues' actions, I slowly started to stretch outside of my comfort zone and refine my own interpersonal skills —initially just by going to lunch with people from different levels of the organization and talking to them about casual topics such as sports, college life, our children, and other interests we shared in common. This grew into exchanging thoughts and ideas about career advancement opportunities, the organization's strategy, pros and cons of different management styles, and who would be good mentors. In the process I discovered that cultivating personal relationships provided me access to information, and insights about the organization, that otherwise I would never have known about.

The reality is that by extending yourself, building social and professional connections, and leveraging personal affiliations, you become more effective.

Relying solely on your individual ability limits what you accomplish. Alternatively, collaborating and being part of a group whose skills complement each other allows you to do more, and achieve more, than you could ever do on your own. By working together, ordinary people can accomplish extraordinary things.

It is important to note, however, that while building a network of relationships has tremendous benefits, you cannot lose sight of the fact that to achieve your goals, you also need to be able to point to what you personally accomplished in conjunction with what the group achieved.

When it comes to developing networks and mutually beneficial relationships, participating in extracurricular activities is one of the best ways to position yourself so you can meet, and speak casually with, people you are attempting to get to know or want to interact with.

In a majority of private secondary schools, especially in the New England area, faculty members coach a sport each day after classes are completed. The primary purpose of these private schools having teachers' coach a sport is not to get the most out of them for the salary they are paid, as many people might initially believe. These teachers coach sports because, in addition to good recreation, it provides the students an opportunity to experience the nuisances of building rapport with people in authority.

Interacting with faculty members in a different setting allows the students to engage in a new way with their teachers, which carry over into the classroom.

Of course, these private schools could retain people not directly associated with the school to coach, but providing the opportunity for students to observe their teachers in a different setting is important — supported by the fact that this private-school tradition enlightens students on the value of leveraging their interpersonal skills in diverse situations.

Extending yourself socially in a strategic way can not only enhance your chances for success by helping you foster new friendships and affiliations, but just as importantly it can also be enjoyable, and personally rewarding.

You can take that first step to enhancing your interpersonal skills by engaging in activities that require you to interact and expand your comfort zone. As a precursor, start by talking to people about topics of mutual interest, which are not controversial or politically sensitive.

For instance, if someone you want to meet, or engage in a conversation with, is an avid baseball fan, scan the sports pages so you can be up-to-date on the latest baseball news. If a colleague is going to a music concert, listen to a few songs from the feature singer/group so you will be able to better connect with him or her.

Establishing relationships with a diverse group of people can be extremely beneficial. However, as you go about building your network you have to choose your associations wisely, and be keenly aware of whom you are befriending.

There is a passage in the Book of Proverbs that states, "He who walks with wise men will be wise, but the companion of fools will suffer harm." Said another way, if you want to excel in any aspect of your life, it makes perfectly good sense to associate with successful people who have already accomplished what you are trying to achieve. On the other hand, if you habitually socialize with people who have a loser's mentality and have not attained anything of importance in their lives, then you are doomed to become just like them.

Although guilty by association may be a cliché, there is no denying successful people tend to associate with other successful people, while underachievers tend to be friends with other underachievers.

Along with leveraging your interpersonal skills, understanding the organizational culture you are operating in is extremely important. To a vast majority of people, "playing politics" is a dirty phrase. In fact many people deny that organization politics, or what I would describe as an informal, or casual, decision-making process, exists.

And, some individuals who acknowledge that organization politics exists will still insist it invokes no role in determining your success, or impacts what you accomplish. Both of these are very naïve and dangerous assumptions to make.

Through my personal and professional life experiences, I have observed that it is inevitable that you will encounter, and have to interact with, people who possess their own personal agendas and motives. And in the process, you will see organization politics exploited for both good and bad purposes.

The secret to being better than your best is to expand your knowledge of organization politics, not deny or ignore it. Comprehending other people's agendas inherently makes you more astute, and places you in a better position to proactively take the appropriate actions, which are required to successfully navigate a path to your own objectives.

Believe it or not, organization politics is in and of itself neutral. It is its application that determines whether or not the ramifications are positive or negative. Therefore, my purpose here is not to opine on whether or not playing organization politics is a good or bad alternative for you. The point is if you understand organization politics and anticipate how it factors into the decision-making process, you can leverage your interpersonal skills appropriately so that organization politics can be utilized to your advantage.

For me, one way of demystifying organization politics is to view it as a series of games. Contemplate this for a moment. You have been in the past, or are currently involved with, an school/college organization, church group, social club, fraternity, sorority, or team of some sort. For each of these organizations there are rules/guidelines that apply, and to reap the benefits of being a member you must understand, and abide by, the prescribed conduct or actions.

In essence, organization politics is about being aware of and adhering to the rules, earning the confidence of people you want to influence, communicating what you know in a manner everybody can understand, and getting others to value your input.

If you observe what is going on around you, and master the subtleties of the various situations you encounter, you are by design more in control of your own destiny. The key in most organizations is discerning what the rules are, especially the ones that are not spoken, or those that are unwritten and based on custom/historical rituals.

While politics in every organization can be a bit unique, here is an example of a few simple yet effective guidelines that might prevent you from making a mishap, which could derail your pursuit of success. And more importantly, mastering these rules could help you play the game a little better than everyone else.

Rules of the Game:

- There is no such thing as a confidential, off-the-record, or private conversation. If there is something you really do not want shared, or anyone else to know about, then you should keep it to yourself. You must always assume *everything* you say or write about someone or something, even if it is shared with someone you trust, will become public knowledge.

- Maintain a positive relationship with everyone, even the people you think do not matter. You never know when you might need an ally or a favor.

- Think before speaking, or sending an e-mail or text message, and always respond with intelligence, not emotion.

- Be viewed as a team player. Have integrity and be thought of as someone who is honest and can be trusted to always do the right thing.

- Know whom the influencers and decision-makers are, and tactfully develop a mutually beneficial relationship.

- Always show up early for work, appointments, practices, and meetings. Never arrive late, or turn in a project beyond the agreed time. "On time" means being early.

- Be visible and sociable in your organization. But also be aware that you are judged by whom you associate with.

- Attend the important organization events. At the same time, understand that your behavior at these functions is being monitored. This is not the appropriate venue to ascertain how much of the free alcohol you can consume.

- Do not be a maverick; focus on the core role that was assigned to you, and do it well, before taking on new, or special, projects trying to make a big impact.

- Keep your personal and professional lives separate, and do not use the organization's time or assets for your own benefit.

- Dress for success, within the confines of the culture, and maintain a professional appearance. An outfit may be perfectly fine for an outing with close personal friends, but totally inappropriate for organization functions.

- Watch, manage, and be keenly aware of what appears on social networks. What happens in Las Vegas may stay in Las Vegas, but pictures of what happened in Las Vegas also stay on YouTube, Twitter, LinkedIn, and Facebook.

- If you are in the wrong place, personally or professionally, take the appropriate actions to maneuver yourself into a better situation. Do not be reluctant or afraid to pursue other opportunities; they will not magically come to you.

- Maintain a network of people you can proactively leverage to keep you aware of what is going on in the organization, and with your career prospects. Also, know what is important to people who can influence your success or failure.

What I have described here is not an exhaustive list. It is just a snapshot of what you need to keep in mind, since not all of the rules you will encounter in an organization are explicit, intellectual, or even applied consistently for that matter. And, while following these guidelines will not guarantee success, they can be extremely beneficial in keeping you on the right path.

In conjunction with organization politics, every organization has decision makers, and those who secretly influence the decision makers. And, it is not always abundantly clear who these various people are, because the person who is officially acknowledged as being in charge is not necessarily the one who makes the ultimate decisions.

In a majority of instances someone influences the decision makers, and that influence can be formal or informal in nature. Being in a leadership position, such as a boss, coach, chairperson, or president for example, carries with it formal legitimate authority to make and/ or influence decisions.

On the other hand, informal power is more clandestine and gained as a result of whom, or what, you know. Furthermore, informal power can be used for the purpose of obtaining influence that vastly exceeds someone's legitimate authority. As a result, there are many occasions when it can be more advantageous to have informal power than formal power.

If you are going to be better than your best, it is vitally important that you recognize the dynamics of organizational power, and know who has the ability to make, or influence, the decisions that can impact your success. Also, be acutely aware that the individuals, who determine and exert control over your success, or failure, can change swiftly in organizations. People who make decisions that can impact what you achieve get promoted, demoted, and leave organizations all of the time. So you have to expand your social and professional networks, and proactively plan for the change, prior to the power shift occurring.

To achieve your goals and objectives you must be astute enough to navigate the organization politics, and utilize your interpersonal skills to sway the influencers, as well as the formal decision makers.

To be crystal clear, when I speak about mastering the rules of the game I do not mean to suggest or convey that you should spend all of your time attempting to manipulate people, or on self-adulation; quite the contrary. Being aware of the organization politics is essential to your being successful, but you must be wise and savvy in the process. If others perceive you are only concerned about benefiting yourself, and are not focused on being a team player and contribut-ing to the greater good, the rules of the game can, and will, be used against you.

Let me give you a practical example. At one point in my career, I remember sitting down with my manager for an annual performance review. After we had gone through all of the requisite aspects of what I had done well, and what he thought I could improve upon, he said to me, "Personally your individual performance during this past year was very good, but in the coming months I would like to see you take the initiative to be more of a team player. Take on projects that will allow you to work more with others and demonstrate how you can add value to the entire organization." How could he suggest I was not adding value when I had accomplished every individual task that was assigned to me?

As I would learn later, adding value is not just about doing your job and only focusing on accomplishing what is expected and asked of you. Adding value is about going above and beyond what is expected, and contributing whatever you can to provide a competitive advan-tage to the entire organization without reverting to the adage "that is not my responsibility," or expecting personal awards and accolades in exchange. You have to be perceived as someone who without be-ing supplicated seeks to do things for everyone's benefit, and is not merely self-serving.

The secret to getting people to acknowledge that you are not preten-tious is constantly performing at a level that makes others look good. In fact, one of the most overlooked ways to be perceived as adding value is to always make your boss/coach/colleague/significant other look good.

It does not matter the environment, be it work, the classroom, your home life, or a team, you have to be perceived as someone who is dedicated to doing what is best for everyone, and not be interested only in yourself, before you can reap the full benefits of being a part of that particular group.

Pause for a moment and contemplate the goals you are striving to achieve. Are you blindly working toward your own personal success with no solicitude for others who could potentially assist you in obtaining what you want? Or are you adding value along the way? By making a positive impact on other people you are simultaneously building a network of allies, and in essence helping yourself.

The truth is, in certain situations you may be better served by choosing to be seen as a supporter, versus a leader. This single act can build others' confidence in you, reassure people that you are a team player, and demonstrate how you can provide value and what you are capable of accomplishing.

If you promote the activities of others along the way, it will serve you well as you pursue your ultimate objectives. You never know from whom, when, or where your support will come, so always be cognizant of how your interpersonal skills impact others. People you have assisted or endorsed might very well, when you least expect it, reciprocate by being an advocate on your behalf.

No matter how well you have done, and what you have achieved up to this point in your life, to a great extent what you accomplish henceforth will depend on how successful you are at leveraging your interpersonal skills.

Theodore "Teddy" Roosevelt, who, among other of his great accomplishments, was the 26th president of the United States, was quoted as saying, "The most important single ingredient in the formula of success is knowing how to get along with people."

You are primed to succeed. Your challenge is to learn how to grasp the nuance of your interpersonal skills while being acutely aware of what is going on around you. Executing these two things will help ensure that as you strive to achieve your dreams, you are deploying all of your positive attributes to their full advantage.

Achieving success is a lot easier if you "Master the Rules of the Game," but along the way do not forget to "Maintain Your Moral Compass."

Maintain Your Moral Compass

Just because someone else is doing something does not make it acceptable or right…

When we were growing up most of us learned our patrician values, as very young children, from our parents, teachers, religious leaders, coaches, and other family members or friends. As adults it is imperative that you revisit those values on a daily basis to ensure you are staying true to your morals.

Being honest, having integrity, conforming to the law, and maintaining respect for others are all an integral part of defining your moral compass.

Mahatma Gandhi was a prominent, and many would say pivotal, figure during India's independence movement against British colonial rule. Gandhi believed in resistance through mass civil disobedience and nonviolence. The concept of disobedience and nonviolence helped India gain its independence, and influenced Dr. Martin Luther King's philosophy that was utilized by black Americans to obtain civil rights in the United States. Gandhi was quoted as saying, "Faith in God is the foundation of all moral values." Gandhi never defined God, and was prepared to allow every person to have his or her own idea of God, but nonetheless he fully understood the importance of having moral values in one's life.

The question you must answer is how do your moral values manifest themselves in your daily life?

As you strive for success, your ambition, and the desire to achieve more, can change the person you are. Therefore, you have to be cognizant of your moral values, and make them the foundation upon which all of your decisions are based.

At some stage achieving the success you desire in your life will require sacrifice and negotiation. And one of the critically important negotiation tools in your quest for success is the art of compromise. But compromising your moral values is a guaranteed detour from which you may never recover.

Therefore, to avoid jeopardizing your moral values I would strongly recommend that you compile a list outlining three things:

- Things that you are compelled to do to obtain what you desire, which are consistent with your moral values.

- Things that you are not completely satisfied doing, but will engage in if necessary to accomplish your goals and objectives.

- Things that you will absolutely never ever do, regardless of the consequences or potential benefits.

Having a defined set of moral values provides clarity to help you make difficult decisions with integrity. And, your values also serve as a moral compass to ensure you stay on the straight and narrow path, and thereby take appropriate actions to obtain the desired results you are seeking.

Both of my sons attended high school at the Brunswick School in Greenwich, Connecticut. Along with providing a challenging academic environment, Brunswick's overriding objective is to foster the development of strong personal character. The school's motto "Courage, Honor, Truth" reinforces this commitment.

By instilling into their students the values of honesty, integrity, and compassion, Brunswick's guiding principles provide a great illustration of how, unless you have a pristine understanding of things you will never do and actions you will never take, you risk violating your moral values and doing something that causes you to spiral out of control.

To be successful at anything in life you need to make your own value-based decisions, and not place your future in someone else's hands. As a result, among the many important decisions you have to make is determining who is worthy of your trust. To avoid engaging in something that you may ultimately regret when you encounter anyone - or are in any situation - that goes against your moral values, I urge you to *run*, not walk, the other way.

Always remember it is not important who people say you are. It is only important that you know who you are and what you stand for — and against.

I alluded in chapter three to mastering the rules of the game, but I want to reiterate there is a monumental difference between playing the game and compromising your values.

Playing the game means you are in charge of what you do, thoroughly understand why you are doing it, and accept complete responsibility for the outcomes.

Compromising your values means you have lost your personal

integrity, and as a result surrendered control of who you are, and what you stand for as a person, to someone else.

To be better than your best and be in charge of your life, you must decide what you want to achieve, both personally and professionally. And, to arrive at that decision you need to be focused, or more specifically, have a well-thought-out plan.

It is rare that someone finds success by aimlessly wandering through life with no particular goals in mind. Success comes to people who make things happen for them, not to those who let things happen to them. And, as the old saying goes, "If you do not know where you are going, any road will get you there."

Successful people understand that they alone are responsible for creating the most out of the challenges and opportunities that present themselves along life's journey.

What you need to be aware of is there are times when you get so preoccupied just living life on a day-to-day basis, you neglect to look up and see where the road you are traveling on is leading you. The danger lies in waking up one day and discovering that where you ended up in life was not your intended destination.

To be successful in any aspect of your life you must determine what your passion is, what you want to accomplish, and how committed you are to doing what it will take to achieve your objectives. Now I do not want to suggest this can be accomplished in isolation. You may have family members, friends, or colleagues that will be impacted by the choices you make. Their respective roles in your life, and your role in their lives, should be consciously factored into your decision-making process.

Therefore, as you pursue your future aspirations, it is critical that you take the time to recognize what is important to those around you. You know what is paramount to you. But others do not see the world through your eyes.

In every situation you encounter you bring along your own personal perspective, which includes your childhood experiences, family dynamics, educational training, past relationships, and professional expertise.

So too do each of your family members, friends, colleagues, associates, and competitors possess their own unique experiences and perspectives. Simply acknowledging the existence of these various differences will provide you with greater insight. However, if you take it a step further and attempt to understand those distinctions, to look at a situation through their eyes, from their perspective, just think of the vast potential you could unleash.

Your prospect for success expands exponentially with the ability to sell your ideas, but with a different pitch, the chance to rally your team using a message that is meaningful to them, and perhaps most importantly, the capability to make an impact in someone's life by simply understanding their needs and motivations.

This is the kind of leadership that not only inspires others to follow, but it makes true believers out of them as well. So the ability to maintain your moral values, be who you are, and at the same time collaborate with people who retain views that are different from you, is critical to your success.

I have stated many times throughout the respective chapters in this book that to be better than your best you have to decide what you want out of life, and take responsibility for making it happen. One of the best techniques to keep you fixated on what is important to you is to have a written plan that clearly details your goals and objectives.

Concurrently having a well-thought-out plan also enables you to pro-actively think ahead and anticipate various scenarios.

Every successful organization has a written annual plan and a long-term strategic plan that delineate their business/financial goals and objectives. If multi-billion-dollar organizations believe it is beneficial to have plans detailing their short - and long - term goals and objec-tives, doesn't it seem rationale for you to have your own personal vision that lays out what success looks like for you?

Far too often people procrastinate and wait until they have limited options, or no other alternatives, before they start to think about plan-ning. Waiting until you are unemployed, financially distressed, a relationship has gone completely bad, or you have run out of time severely curtails the possible actions you could have initiated. The time to make a change, or plan for a change, is when your ability to choose or decide is the greatest, not when you are under pressure and forced to make a change. You have to anticipate what is forthcoming and get prepared before it happens.

I cannot begin to tell you how many people call me after they have been displaced from their job wanting my guidance and assistance. My first reaction is, was this a surprise, or did you see the impending signs and neglect to act?

Normally all of the signals foretelling what is about to happen are there and you just fail to see them. Or worst yet, you see them and do not put an action plan in place to deal with a situation that is inevi-table. The time to pursue different alternatives, update your resume, make new relationships, save money, or change your course of action is when you have ample opportunities, options, and resources on your side, not when you are desperate.

You are at your best when you have the time and competency to think, prepare, and act intelligently. Waiting until situations are at their worst, before you undertake any action, is never as effective as making decisions when you have time on your side. Time is the most valuable resource you possess. You can make more money, but you cannot extend the hours in the day and procure more time. Therefore, to be better than your best you have to be proactive, anticipate what is coming, and plan ahead. Where and how you invest your precious time will play a significant role in determining your success.

I recognize that taking the time to develop a written plan can seem boring and mundane. However, effective planning is an essential ingredient that separates the winners from the losers. Having a detailed, well-thought-out plan for your intellectual independence allows you to effectively schedule, plot, and strategize your next exploits so you do not become overwhelmed, or frustrated, by the tasks that lie ahead. Trust me, if you do not take the time upfront to consciously plan, and use priorities to guide your actions, the odds for achieving success are against you. Without a roadmap delineating what you want to accomplish, and what actions are required, you will drift off course, and ultimately not achieve your desired results. And, while falling short of the plans you lay out may be disappointing, not having any plans or objectives is a disaster waiting to happen.

To achieve any meaningful level of success and derive significant accomplishments, you have to view yourself as your own personal enterprise and have a written plan — the key words being *"written plan"* — outlining what you want to achieve and how you intend to obtain it.

The primary reason I stress putting your plan in writing is because it forces you to reflect upon, and internalize, your thoughts. If you are like most people when someone asks if you have a plan for your life, you will respond, "Yes, it's all in my head." When your goals are in your head they are not plans, they are just an idea. Writing down your personal objectives assists you in formulating your thinking, and the goals become crystallized and actionable.

Also, keeping your goals in front of you at all times, and seeing them in writing, will serve as a constant reminder of what you are striving to achieve — thereby helping to preclude you from doing something that might derail you from accomplishing your ultimate objectives.

Besides, rushing into something without thinking it completely through can, and often does, lead to results that are less than stellar.

Maintaining a written plan of your goals and objectives gives you a personal guidebook to continuously refer back to. And, your written plan will assist in keeping you concentrated on what is important, and what you may need to change or adjust along the way.

Proactively thinking through where you are currently in your life, what you are trying to accomplish, and what steps are necessary to get you where you want to be, will serve you far better than irrationally reacting to a situation when it occurs.

It does not matter whether your goal is to change careers, start your own business, retire at an early age, improve your health, learn a new language, or repair a strained relationship, to have a decent chance at achieving your goal you need a detailed written plan.

Before you go any further in this book I encourage you to stop, reflect on what it is you want to accomplish, and prepare your personal written plan to meet that objective. And to help you get started here are a few questions you may want to consider asking yourself as you are developing your plan.

Questions to consider when writing your personal plan:

- Who, or what, is most important to you in your life?

- What facets of your life do you need to change or discontinue doing, and what things do you need to start doing, to put you on a clearer path to success?

- What are your short-term goals?

- What specific actions will be required to achieve your short-term goals?

- What are your long-term aspirations?

- What obstacles will detour you from fulfilling your long-term aspirations?

- Are your goals and aspirations consistent with your moral values?

- Are you 100% committed to doing whatever it takes to achieve your goals and aspirations?

- Who else is affected by your decisions, goals, and aspirations?

- Are the people who will be impacted by your plan an enabler, or a deterrent, to your success?

- Do you have people in your life that can be, and are willing to be, helpful to you in achieving your goals and aspirations?

- What is your backup plan, just in case your original plan does not materialize?

Developing an effective personal plan will unequivocally enable you to establish and achieve goals that will contribute to you enjoying a successful, happy and fulfilled life.

A critical, and often overlooked, step in the process of developing a personal plan is determining a realistic time line for achieving the plan. It is imperative that you do not assume you can accomplish something in a day or week that will realistically take months or years.

And, the most important aspect of any plan is that you need to seriously determine if the intrinsic price you are going to incur for your success is worth it, and if you are candidly willing to do whatever it takes to accomplish your goals.

If the goals you outline in your plan are worthwhile and align with your moral values, you have to put all of your energy, focus, and efforts into accomplishing those goals. On the other hand, if the sacrifice, time, and personal commitment are not truly something you have a passion for, or if the pursuit of your goals will cause you to violate your moral values, you need to modify your plan.

Staying true to your goals can be extremely rewarding, and fulfillment cannot be achieved through compromised values, but inevitably, at some point in time, the moral values you have acquired over the course of your lifetime will get challenged. And, unless you have a solid moral foundation, you can begin to question who you are as a person and what you stand for.

A man who I have a tremendous amount of respect for is Larry Thompson. At one point in his illustrious career, Larry served as deputy attorney general in the United States Department of Justice under then President George W. Bush.

While Deputy United States Attorney General Larry led the efforts to punish white-collar crime. Among other notable accomplishments he oversaw prosecutions against officials at Enron for the scandal that led to the bankruptcy of Enron Corporation, which at the time it occurred was the largest bankruptcy reorganization in American history.

I once inquired of Larry what advice he would give someone concerning his or her personal integrity. His response was, "Always be honest. Do what you say you are going to do, and always make certain that in doing what you are supposed to be doing, that you do not cheat or hurt anyone else in the process."

Larry went on to say, "The most important thing that you are going to have at the end of the day are your personal values, and the only thing that is really going to hold you in good stead, as you move on in life, is not really whether you did this assignment or whether you did that assignment, or even whether you did an assignment better than someone else. It is going to be: Is this person someone that we can trust? Is this person someone that we can rely on? And, is this person someone we would like to work with? Above everything else the thing that you have to preserve is your reputation, and a lot of people do not understand that."

As Larry Thompson so eloquently articulated, your reputation is your most important asset, and your word is your bond. So no matter what is asked of you, and how valuable the reward appears, you must always make choices with your eyes wide open. Know the consequences of your actions, and maintain a clear sense of your personal self-worth. Being ethical is extremely important and you must always avoid even the appearance of impropriety.

The fact of the matter is we live in a complex world where ethical issues are not black and white. Everything you do will be judged in hindsight. Actions you take, or a decision you make, may be a judgment call when it happens, but you have to be cognizant of how your choices will be viewed when more details are available and calmer heads prevail.

Whether you realize it or not, every aspect of your life is a reflection of what kind of person you are, and what you stand for — and against.

How you conduct yourself, the questions you ask, your professional appearance, and the people you associate with, all contribute to defining how other people perceive you.

Therefore, when you encounter a situation that does not seem right, or you are at a crossroads wondering what you should do, you need to stop and think of the people in your life whom you respect the most, and ask yourself what they would do in this instance. How would they handle this particular situation? What would they tell you if they were standing there with you?

A moral gauge I have used throughout my life is the "full disclosure" test. If what I was about to do was broadcast across the Internet for all of my family, friends, and colleagues to see, would I be proud or embarrassed?

If the answer was ashamed and embarrassed, or I had serious doubts about right versus wrong, I tried to always take the higher ground and erred on the safe, conservative side. Holding yourself to a higher standard than anyone else expects will always prove to be advantageous in whatever endeavor you pursue.

While taking an unpopular stance, and standing by your principles, is not always easy, in the end staying true to your moral compass is a far greater reward than any benefit that comes from making choices you are not comfortable with.

Believe me, it does not matter what other people say or do; your faith, and belief in yourself, is your strongest asset. So you have to decide what you want out of your life, determine if you are willing to pay the personal price to achieve it, and always, and I do mean always, stay true to your moral values.

And one of the best ways to "Maintain Your Moral Compass" is to "Get Honest Feedback."

CHAPTER Five

Get Honest Feedback

Trusting people is important, but make sure to verify what you are being told...

Being self-aware of your strengths and opportunity areas is a fundamental attribute that is required to be better than your best. As a matter of fact, in order to proceed on the path to making positive changes in your life you initially have to be aware of the things you want, or need, to change.

While you can alter the behaviors you are cognizant of, the real insight emerges from becoming aware of the obstacles you did not realize were hindering your personal growth. Therefore, getting honest, objective feedback will serve you extensively better than surrounding yourself with people who always agree with you.

"The Emperor's New Clothes" by Hans Christian Andersen is a classic tale. It is also a great illustration of someone who was not self-aware and as a result convinced himself, and the people closest to him, to believe in something that did not exist. Worst yet, individuals he trusted did not provide honest input, making the situation even more absurd.

The story revolves around two weavers who promise an emperor a new suit of clothes from a fabric they claim is invisible to anyone who is incompetent, or just hopelessly dense.

In actuality neither the emperor, nor his closest advisors, could see the cloth themselves, but they allege they can out of fear of appearing unintelligent or unfit for their positions.

When the two con men report the suit is finished they feign dressing the emperor, who then parades before his subjects. A child in the crowd calls out, "The Emperor is not wearing any clothes." The emperor cringes', suspecting what the child said is true, but nonetheless proudly continues the procession.

The moral of the story is that convincing yourself to believe in something that you know, or all the facts suggest, is not true, and taking counsel or advice from someone who always agrees with you, will be pernicious and can hinder your success.

To get an honest assessment of any situation you need to develop a sphere of confidants who will be honest and provide you with balanced, objective feedback.

I will readily admit that being surrounded by family, friends, and colleagues who love and support you, no matter the situation or circumstance, can be beneficial in certain instances. But, at the same time, you do not want everyone in your inner circle to mimic your actions and only tell you what they believe you want to hear.

Entrusting your success with "yes men" or "yes women" who do not provide you with independent, intelligent, guidance is a recipe for disaster. Worst yet, it is a proven fact that people who will lie for you will lie to you.

While it is extremely important to associate with people who will be honest with you, at the same time, you have to guard against placing people in your life who have the same opportunity areas that you possess.

It may be accurate that people who have similar issues can provide moral support for each other, but it is also true that people who have diverse experiences, varied skills, and different points of view formulate the most creative solutions to difficult problems.

Although it is not always easy to do, to be better than your best, you have to learn to value input from people who are dispensing feedback and perspectives you do not want to acknowledge, or do not always concur with.

Let me be perfectly clear. There is a distinct difference between courteous, respectful comments and ill-conceived criticism. I personally do not accept the notion that criticism provides any intrinsic value. While positive, well-intended feedback can broaden your outlook and challenge your thought process, criticism merely serves the purpose of trying to undermine your self-esteem.

Nevertheless, rather than being paranoid and discounting everything a person who has a different point of view says, you will be better served if you take the comments, analyze them, and determine if they have any redeeming value that you can utilize. This is not to suggest that all of the opinions and reactions you receive will be valuable, or that you have to agree with, or accept, what is being said. The lesson to be learned is that you need to make sure not to ignore or reject constructive two-way communication that may in fact be a valuable learning opportunity.

Procuring clear, objective feedback can be difficult, mainly because most of the people you approach to obtain feedback from want to be seen as being supportive, and do not want to jeopardize their relationship with you. Therefore, you are often faced with the dilemma of choosing between people who will give you their biased opinions or filtered feedback, and those who will provide an honest, independent assessment.

Having someone who will always see the best in you and give you positive reinforcement serves a valid purpose, and there are definitely times when you need someone to pick up your spirits and make you feel better. On the other hand, getting blunt, issue-specific feedback does not always make you feel good, and may be difficult to accept. However, at the end of the day getting honest, timely, direct feedback provides you with valuable insights that will help you achieve your objectives.

Here are a few tips that you can employ to assist you in establishing a process for obtaining honest feedback.

Tips on How to Obtain Honest Feedback:

- Make a list of the people you genuinely trust and can openly share issues and concerns with. Keep in mind that the people you admire and respect will change over time as your life evolves.

- When you seek feedback, be open to receiving ideas and suggestions that do not align with your way of thinking. Even if the comments are not useful, if you respond negatively people will be less likely to offer their input the next time.

- Get information, and different points of view, from as many people as possible to corroborate what is being said.

- Foster an ongoing relationship that encourages people to feel compelled to have a shared responsibility in your success.

- Be objective about your strengths and opportunity areas, and be prepared to communicate the complete story with people you are seeking advice from. If you are not at ease sharing with people you are asking assistance from, odds are they will not be comfortable providing feedback.

- Test people to determine if they can be trusted. At the same time you cannot become so paranoid that you do not have confidence in anyone.

- Do not rely solely on family members, or close personal friends, for advice and feedback. The people closest to you may know you the best, but they can also be less objective when it comes to providing unbiased points of view.

- Read between the lines and focus on what is not being said, and what people do, just as much as you focus on what is being said. Actions do in fact speak louder than words.

On your journey to being better than your best, be aware that along with meeting people who will be instrumental in your success, you will also encounter people who are going to attempt to derail your dreams and aspirations.

Some of these people will be well intended, and think they are being a good friend who is saving you from the disappointment of having big goals and aspirations that *they* do not think you can accomplish. I call these people "dream killers." Dream killers do not have faith in you and your abilities, and believe you will fail and not fulfill your dreams. So by preventing you from pursuing your goals, dream killers are of the opinion that they are saving you from failure.

Alternatively, there is also a cadre of people who are more devious and cannot envision the thought of you doing more, achieving more, and receiving more than them.

People like this will articulate awful things about your character, and will gossip, cheat, and lie to you, or on you. Their actions are meant to hurt, discourage, and cause you malaise. These people are "haters" and have a "what makes you think you are better than me" mentality. And, haters will do everything in their limited power to prevent you from succeeding.

It will not be easy, however the dream killers and haters who manifest themselves in your life need to be avoided at all cost. Your challenge is to identify and surround yourself with supportive people who will encourage you, and provide honest advice, as you face the trials and tribulations that will enviably come about as you strive to make positive changes.

The good news is, while interactions with people who do not support you and your dreams can momentarily slow you down, if you have faith and put the teaching from this book to work in your life, nothing will prevent you from achieving your dreams and aspirations.

Irrespective of your religious beliefs, there is a passage in the Old Testament that will serve you well as you confront the obstacles placed in your path.

Isaiah 54:17 - "No weapon that is formed against you will prosper." In other words no person, situation, or circumstance that stands in the way of your being better than your best will succeed. This is not to suggest things people say and do might not temporarily affect you; however, they ultimately will not be victorious. You are a conqueror and a winner. And, although you may endure some momentary setbacks, in the process you will become stronger and wiser, and ultimately prevail.

One of the best ways to maneuver around the challenges placed in your path is to establish a mentor-protégé relationship with someone who possesses the wisdom, experience, and skills that you desire and can benefit from.

Most successful people acknowledge that having a mentor is essential as you navigate a course toward your goals. They also understand that establishing a true mentor-protégé relationship involves confession of your insufficiencies and acknowledgement that you need assistance.

It takes real maturity to seek out and establish strong mentoring relationships with people who you can trust. And, when you take that important step, you demonstrate even more sophistication by being open to considering ideas, and recommendations, that do not always align with your preconceived way of thinking.

Many people do not succeed in acquiring the appropriate mentor(s) because they underestimate the time and effort required to establish the proper mentor-protégé relationship. Procuring a suitable mentor can be a dubious task, and the attributes you are seeking may not be fully contained in any one person, resulting in your requiring multiple mentors.

Along with all of the other characteristics you may personally desire in a mentor, I strongly suggest seeking a mentor who is someone you respect and admire, and someone who believes in you and the tremendous potential you possess.

While mentor relationships can by design be formal or informal in nature, every successful individual I know has a person, or persons, in their life that they have a strong formal mentoring relationship with.

I have ascertained that if you are sincere, and approach your potential mentor in a positive manner, most people want to help, and take it as a compliment that you asked for and value their guidance.

I would be remiss if I failed to mention that merely having a mentor does not guarantee success. However, placing people in your life who are willing to invest their time, talents, and resourcefulness in helping you build your future is a huge advantage.

One of the classic examples of a beneficial mentor-protégé relationship is found in the popular movie *The Karate Kid*. *The Karate Kid* is about a teenager who moves to a new city and almost immediately finds himself the target of bullies. The boy's initial inclination is to simply try to avoid the bullies. Yet, after learning that he shares an apartment building with an aging karate master, he agrees to train and be mentored by the man so he can compete in a karate tournament against his nemesis.

A memorable scene in the movie occurs during one of their training sessions when the karate master is instructing/mentoring the boy on how to wax his car. The young protégé feels frustrated, believing this task has nothing to do with karate and is all about the karate master getting him to shine his car. In actuality the wise mentor is using this process to teach muscle memory and karate techniques, which results in the protégé winning the karate tournament.

Ultimately it is the mentorship of the karate master, including his words of wisdom, hands-on approach, and the time he spends with the boy that makes the difference.

The Karate Kid is an excellent metaphor of good triumphing over evil and finding your inner strength to achieve your goals. On the other hand, it also highlights some of the key components of a successful mentor-protégé relationship, including trust, commitment, mutual respect, honest communication, and the willingness to work through obstacles.

While having a mentor is paramount for success, to be effective a good mentor-protégé relationship cannot be one where all you do is "take," and do not "give" in return. The best mentor-protégé relationships are mutually beneficial for the mentor and protégé. And, at various times, they learn something from each other.

Therefore, when you establish your mentor-protégé relationship, strive hard to make certain it is not merely a one-sided affair. As a protégé you may be able to provide information and insights that are valuable to the mentor. Or you may be able to make introductions, which expand your mentor's network of colleagues and friends. No matter the situation, always try to make the relationship mutually beneficial so both parties feel good about the connection.

The essence of a meaningful mentoring relationship is the ability of the mentor to see and communicate the big picture, while the protégé is immersed in the day-to-day realities of trying to accomplish his or her objectives.

Determining all of the actions required to achieve your objectives can be excruciating. Therefore, it can be extremely beneficial to have another person who has a shared interest in your success provide an unbiased point of view.

While you are in the process of striving to reach your goals it is also important to maintain an ongoing relationship with your mentors. Do not wait until you have a problem, or need your mentor's support, before you reach out to him or her.

One of the biggest mistakes people make in various aspects of their lives is being ashamed or afraid to ask for guidance, or waiting until it is too late before admitting they need assistance. Some people feel that asking questions or admitting they do not know something is a sign of weakness. To the contrary, being willing and able to admit what you do not know, and asking for assistance, is a sign of self-awareness and confidence—both of which are important aspects to your obtaining success and happiness.

Albert Einstein, who is regarded as one of the most prolific intellects in human history, once said, "The important thing is not to stop questioning. Curiosity has its own reason for existing. One cannot help but be in awe when he contemplates the mysteries of eternity, of life, of the marvelous structure of reality."

So stay in touch with your mentors on a routine basis, share the good and bad news, ask questions, and make them feel a part of your journey. That way when you have a problem, or need their guidance, the communication lines between you and your mentor will already be established.

Another valuable lesson to learn is that there is a distinct difference between having a mentor and someone being your sponsor. Some people think the terms are interchangeable, but according to the American Heritage Dictionary a mentor is "a wise and trusted counselor or teacher," while a sponsor is "one who assumes responsibility for another person."

In other words, a mentor can answer your questions and advises you on how to navigate the challenges you are facing, while a sponsor sells your abilities to others and is an advocate to help you obtain the success you are seeking.

Although it is not always the case, your mentor and sponsor can be comprised in the same person. David B. Rickard, who retired as Executive Vice President, Chief Financial Officer, and Chief Administrative Officer of CVS Caremark Corporation, is a mentor to me, as well as, one of my staunchest sponsors. David explains it this way: "The difference between a mentor and a sponsor is who the audience is. Mentoring is advising/coaching the individual. Sponsoring is working with others in the interest of the individual, as in rec-ommending the individual for a specific job or promotion. I have probably mentored dozens, or even hundreds, of people. But I have always viewed my job as a manager or executive as being responsible for sponsoring all the people in my group, in relation to their abilities and interests."

It is not uncommon for influential people to have someone they share an interest in, take under their wing, or assume responsibility and vouch for. Maybe the person reminds them of himself or herself, or perhaps they just see attributes in the person that encourages them to want to be an advocate.

In any case, the influential person takes it upon him - or her - self to communicate on behalf of, or "sponsor," this individual, normally without the person even knowing.

While you can and should actively solicit and persuade a person to be your mentor, a sponsorship is more personal and discreet. You normally cannot induce a person to be an advocate for you if they are not already so inclined.

Sponsors can be invaluable in helping you navigate through the obstacles and challenges, while also creating opportunities that nor-mally would not be available to you. And, although you should not openly petition for their support, be exemplary in everything you do, and maintain a relationship of respect, and professionalism, with in-dividuals you sense could be potential sponsors.

While it is prudent, and recommended, to actively seek out and acknowledge someone as your mentor, the same guidelines do not apply for sponsors. You should not constantly apprise someone that you consider them a "sponsor," because they might assume you had ulterior motives for establishing a relationship with them. As a result they might not advocate on your behalf when they otherwise might have been so inclined.

The lessons to be learned from all of this are that to be better than your best and succeed in any aspect of your life, you have to be surrounded by objective, supportive people who along with being honest are well intended and have your best interest at heart.

Make sure you always "Get Honest Feedback" and develop a network of capable people who assume a shared responsibility for your success, but in addition to doing that you also must "Invest in What You Are Doing."

CHAPTER Six

Invest in What You Are Doing

It is not about the money, it is about the respect…

Achieving success is a journey, and if you want to enhance your future you must be willing to devote the time and attention that is necessary to attain what you are attempting to accomplish.

Among other things, being better than your best means going beyond what other people would consider normal, and developing new patterns of behavior that are consistent with the goals you want to accomplish. Consequently, if you do not proactively put forth the unrelenting effort required to attain your objectives, and instead just sit on your derriere passively waiting for success and happiness to come to you, all you will end up with is disappointment and sore buttocks.

When you watch professional athletes perform, they appear to make the difficult seem easy, yet you may neglect to comprehend the number of hours, days, weeks, months, and years they have spent perfecting their skills.

Professional Football Hall of Fame wide receiver Jerry Rice epitomizes the concept that with desire, determination, and dedication you can achieve tremendous success.

Although Rice was undoubtedly talented he was not blessed with the fastest speed, or the most natural football abilities. Even Rice himself would probably agree that some of the other players who occupied his position were more gifted athletes. Nevertheless, Jerry Rice is regarded as the greatest wide receiver to ever play in the National Football League.

Why is Jerry Rice considered the best? Undoubtedly it is a result of his unbelievable work ethic and positive attitude that nobody was going to work harder, be better conditioned, better prepared mentally, or compete more intensely than he did.

During the off-season when other players would relax, play golf, and take a break away from football, Rice was working out, running, lifting weights, and studying film. It was not always fun, but Rice knew there is no easy road to success. And, along with investing the time and effort required to be the best, Rice was willing to make sacrifices to achieve his objectives.

While you may not be like Jerry Rice on the football field you can emulate his work ethic, and dedication to success, in other aspects of your life.

The time you devote today toward attaining your goals may not fully manifest itself tomorrow, or the next day, or even in the next year. However, if you continuously invest in what you are striving to accomplish your toiling will pay off. And eventually you will achieve your dreams and be justly rewarded for all of your commitment and dedication.

Jerry Rice, and people like him who understand the importance of proactively investing the time and extra effort required to be successful, exemplify the famous quote by Admiral Hyman Rickover: "The more you sweat in peace, the less you bleed in war."

Every positive deed you engage in is another building block toward achieving your goals. And, all of the personal sacrifices you put forth today set you up for favorable outcomes in the future. Losers have an off-season, while winners are constantly striving to be better than their best.

The issue with most people is they want instant gratification. And when they do not see immediate results they become frustrated, and stop putting forth the diligence, and perseverance, that will eventually result in them achieving their objectives.

We all know someone who has pursued a foreign language class, or taken private tennis lessons, only to become discouraged at the end of the first series of sessions because they are not conversant in Mandarin, or prepared to join the pro tennis circuit. While their goals could undoubtedly be considered ambitious, the real truth is they did not achieve their lofty expectations because they failed to comprehend, and fully appreciate, the dedication that would be necessary to reach their objectives. They were not in it for the long haul, and therefore were unwilling to devote the requisite amount of time that was mandatory for attaining success. Seeking instant gratification, or the aptly named "quick fix," in any facet of your life is counterproductive to your achieving your long-term goals.

Scientific studies have confirmed that emotionally in your brain, it takes about thirty days to establish a new habit or break an old one.

Thirty days can seem like a lifetime, and the reality is most people never make it to that milestone because, when attempting to make a change, they start and stop, start and stop, always ending up short of their desired outcome.

The secret is that if you are going to make a change you need to do it a little at a time, so you can see some positive results and use the momentum from the small outcomes to propel you to the next phase of the change.

Let's say, for example, that you want to exercise for an hour every day and, due to your schedule, the only available time you have is in the morning. Consequently, you need to wake up earlier than normal to accomplish your objective. Rather than starting tomorrow morning forcing yourself to struggle out of bed an hour early, which, regardless of how hard you try, you know you will not sustain, start by waking up fifteen minutes earlier, and going to bed fifteen minutes earlier at night. When you have established the fifteen minutes as a habit, transition to thirty minutes. Establish the thirty minutes as a habit, and then transition to forty-five minutes. Continue increasing the time until you achieve your ultimate goal of rising an hour earlier than normal.

As I mentioned previously, the dramatic results from the effort you put forth today may not manifest themselves immediately, but that does not mean what you do today does not have a purpose in the pursuit of your long-term goals. Great accomplishments start with small achievements.

Commencing the changes you want to make, by first achieving small goals, will help you build the foundation of knowledge, stamina, and endurance, which will eventually result in your accomplishing your bigger goals.

Also, when you contemplate engaging in any project, objective, or change in your life, make sure what you are doing is consistent with your personal plan, and is something that is important and meaningful to you. Investing your time and energy in something because you feel it is what others believe is best for you, or doing anything that your heart is not into, will not be sustainable, and leads to heartbreak and sadness, versus success and happiness.

One such example of doing something that my heart was not into occurred during a point in my professional career when I was considering changing jobs, primarily because another organization was willing to give me a ten percent increase in my salary. The fact is at that particular time I was happy in my current role, had progressed nicely in my career, and along the way had built an effective network of colleagues who were interested in helping me achieve my long-term goals. While I was not totally convinced that taking the new role was the right move for me, I had a few people who encouraged me to accept the position and "take the money."

So I chased the money and accepted the new job offer. Almost immediately after joining the other organization, I realized I had made a monumental mistake. Not only did I detest the role I was in, but also the people, culture, and work environment were not conducive to helping me achieve my long-term goals. I was miserable, and my less-than-stellar disposition began to infiltrate other areas of my life.

As fate would have it, I reached out to one of my mentors and he confirmed that taking the other job, while it did pay more money in the short-term, was actually a detour away from my long-term goals and aspirations. Fortunately by quickly owning up to my mistake, I was able to make amends and return to a role with my former organization.

Reflecting back on that particular episode I realized I had made a terrible short-term decision that was entirely based on the salary increase, and in the process I did not stop and take the time to think about how misaligned it was with my personal plan. I failed to contemplate whether or not the new role was consistent with my long-term goals, or consider the impact on the personal equity and business relationships I would be leaving behind. The truth is, I did not even consider whether I would be committed to doing my best in the new role.

From that single experience I learned the decisions and choices you make in life should never be purely about money. When you consider making any change in your life, you first need to factor into the equation what you enjoy doing, as well as what you are good and are not good at. If you do something that you enjoy, and make the appropriate decisions that set you up for success, the monetary rewards will eventually come to you.

In fact, there may be times when pursuing an unpaid internship, or taking a lower paying job that is providing experience or exposure consistent with your long-term plan, will serve you far better than accepting a role, you know in your heart you are not interested in, merely for the money.

Now, before you leap to the conclusion that I am suggesting you should *never* be concerned about how much you are getting compensated for your services, let me make myself perfectly clear. You absolutely should not pass up any, and every, opportunity to enhance your financial well-being. You will undoubtedly be confronted with great opportunities that align with your long-term plans, where the benefits of "taking the money" far exceed the downsides. And, in those instances you should not only accept, but insist upon getting, the appropriate remuneration.

Keep in mind, however, that for successful people it is not always about the money. Benjamin Franklin, who was one of the founding fathers of the United States, said, "He that is of the opinion money will do everything may well be suspected of doing everything for money." Anybody can make money, but it takes a special person to make a difference. Therefore, stay true to your personal plan. The money, rewards, and accolades will come once all of the other attributes for your success and happiness are aligned.

I will readily admit that as a result of my being an ambitious person there were a few occasions over the course of my life when I became frustrated and impatience with how things were progressing - or not progressing to be more precise - and I would begin to frantically pursue other opportunities. During one of those occasions I remember speaking to a mentor about my dilemma and he gave me some great advise: "When you make a change make sure you are running toward a situation that is better than the one you are in today, versus running away from a situation because you are caught up in the moment."

My mentor helped me to understand that the time to leave an organization, a relationship, or any situation, is not when you are mad, angry, or frustrated. The time to make a change in any aspect of your life is when you do not foresee a bright future or no longer have the passion and desire that will be required to achieve a meaningful result.

So my advice to you is, when you find yourself getting discouraged and frustrated by the situation you are in, always try to stay focused on what you are going to, "your long-term goals," not what you are going through, "your short-term sacrifices." Otherwise you will make bad decisions, and could end up in a predicament that is far worse than the one you are currently in.

While there are many factors that can cause you to make bad decisions in your life, here are a few of the most prevalent ones.

Things that can cause you to make bad decisions:

- Instead of formulating your decisions based on what you know and think is best, you default to what others are saying or doing. You convince yourself that if everybody else is doing something, or thinks it is okay, it must be right. This is known as succumbing to peer pressure, and it will almost certainly lead to your making a bad decision.

- Reverting to the "I have come this far so I might as well continue" approach. This is the "sunk cost" theory, which means that since you cannot get the time, resources, or money you have previously invested back you might as well continue, even though the odds are stacked against you. The fact of the matter is you have to know when to stop and change directions or approaches.

- Trying to prove that you are correct or smarter than everyone else. Successful people understand that they cannot, and do not, know everything. Therefore, they do not let their egos push them into doing something just to prove a point.

- Failing to analyze your performance, and seek feedback on how you can improve or get better. Successful people obtain guidance and insights from people who can help them get to where they want to be.

- Being impatience or overly confident and not taking the required precautionary steps. Investing the appropriate time and energy to fully understand the situation, and knowing what your plans are before you start something, might prevent you from being sorry later.

- Assuming another person is a moron, or making a presumption about someone that you do not know to be a fact. While you may not always understand their motives or logic, you should never underestimate anyone or their ability to impact what you are attempting to achieve.

In addition to the above points you also need to be mature, and not become so focused on your emotions that you make a bad decision because you fail to see the bigger picture.

Avoiding bad decisions is not easy, but if you can at least be aware of the signs that indicate you are going astray, it will keep you focused as you travel the pathway to your ultimate goals.

Another important lesson I have learned is that if you want someone to support you and invest in your future, you have to be perceived as a team player who is interested in adding value to, investing in, and building equity with that person.

Most people will only invest their time, resources, and effort on you if they believe you are committed and that it is a mutually beneficial relationship. Therefore, make sure that while you are getting what you want, others are also obtaining something they desire. Creating win/win situations will benefit you and contribute to your success.

I would also strongly advise you to take every opportunity to learn and build new skills that will enhance your value and importance. Taking a course or attending conferences and seminars on subjects that enhance your expertise, and volunteering your time to teach or speak to others, are all great ways to invest in, and expand, your knowledge base. At the same time these experiences will provide you an opportunity to network with people, and make new contacts that may prove beneficial in achieving your objectives. And, by investing in yourself you are increasing your value to others in the process.

One of the best ways to enhance your value is to be seen as a problem solver. Perhaps you have heard the old saying, "You are either part of the problem or part of the solution." That is a reality in every facet of your life, and if you have not already learned it, you will soon enough discover, regardless of the situation, that no one likes a problem or a problem maker.

Therefore, no matter what it is you are trying to accomplish, make sure you are perceived as a problem solver and not a problem.

My youngest son enjoys studying mathematics, biology, and chemistry, primarily because each of these academic fields requires an aspect of problem solving.

Assuredly the problems you encounter on a day-to-day basis may not be exactly like the theoretical ones my son enjoys. However, there are a few tricks you can learn by following a simple problem-solving model.

Steps to Problem Solving:

- Maintain a positive attitude and be confident that if you are careful, and persistent, in analyzing the circumstances and situations, it will result in your developing a viable solution.

- Take the time to ensure your initial observations are accurate by learning and understanding the facts, relationships, and interdependencies. Go back and reassess everything as necessary to confirm your conclusions.

- Break the problem down into smaller pieces. Evaluate and make sense of the small pieces, and then proceed from there.

- Avoid guessing and jumping to conclusions without having all of the facts and going through all of the appropriate steps.

- Actively pursue different alternatives and approaches to solve the problem.

Solving problems is not easy; however, the greatest accolades, recognition, and monetary rewards routinely go to people who solve the biggest problems.

Another secret to being better than your best is you have to take prudent risks. The old notion of keeping your head down, and not making a noticeable difference, will not get you to the top. In fact, if you keep your head down you will more than likely not see what is coming, and the opportunity for success will pass by without you even knowing it.

Speaking of taking prudent risks, I mentored a few people when I worked at PepsiCo who were uncomfortable attending business meetings where senior executives would be in attendance. My pro-tégés felt awkward, uncomfortable, and at times petrified in these environments, and were not always quite sure how to conduct them-selves with the senior executives. In essence, going to these meetings was not in their comfort zone, and they actively sought out reasons not to attend.

What some of my mentees failed to comprehend was that by avoiding the opportunity to interact with senior executives, they were limit-ing their exposure to people and resources that could be valuable in helping them achieve their objectives. It is quite natural in meetings where influential people are in attendance not to want to say or do anything that might be embarrassing. But there is a delicate balance you have to maintain. Staying silent, and not speaking up, can be construed as a lack of interest or knowledge. On the other hand, talk-ing too much can be seen as egotistical and self-serving.

My advice when you are in any situations where you feel uncomfort-able or self-conscious is to relax and act as if you belong there as an invited guest. The solution in this particular example is for you to embrace the opportunity to step out of your comfort zone. Introduce yourself, and if given the opportunity talk about a subject you know they are interested in. At the same time, you have to be prepared to demonstrate where you have added value and made a contribution.

An important aspect of how well you do in any aspect of your life will be predicated on making the right choices and taking prudent risks. As I alluded in chapter one, you are the only person who is complete-ly responsible for your success, so hold yourself accountable for your actions, and do not let the fear of taking risks prevent you from staying focused on your goals. Here are some principles I adhere to when I am confronted with the question of whether or not to take a risk.

Guiding principles for taking calculated risks:

- Always evaluate the pros and cons. Do the rewards, benefits, or advantages you can gain by taking the risk outweigh the potential downsides? Also, is what you have to do in taking the risk consistent with your moral compass?

- Make sure taking the risk will solve a real problem. In the scheme of things, does taking the risk significantly matter in determining whether you succeed, or will it only have a minimal impact?

- Make sure the risk aligns with and accentuates your overall plan. Are you doing something that is necessary and consistent with helping you achieve your long-term goals and objectives?

- Fully understand the consequences of the risk you are about to undertake.

- There is a time to act: when you know the chance for success is high and your action plan is sound.

- There is a time to wait and listen: when people are not ready for what you are proposing and you want to reserve the ability to come back and fight another day.

- There is a time to stop: when you are not convinced the odds for success are high and you want, or need, the opportunity to learn more before proceeding.

Also, when you take risks, always attempt to leverage your strengths and minimize your weaknesses. No matter what you are attempting to accomplish, know whether taking the risk is prudent or not, and always try to play to your strengths.

Successful people, like precious diamonds, are formed under extreme pressure and circumstances. So regardless of the obstacles you encounter, you have to make a significant difference and be perceived as a change agent.

Devoting the time necessary to perfect your skills, possessing an unbelievable work ethic, taking calculated risks, and being a problem solver are all critical components which are essential for you to be better than your best. Therefore, as you pursue your goals and aspirations always "Invest in What You Are Doing" and "Negotiate to Get What You Want."

CHAPTER Seven

Negotiate to Get What You Want

The only rule is there are no rules…

You might wonder why I would choose to use the term "negotiate" when it comes to pursuing the goals you have established to get what you want.

Whether you realize it or not, almost every time you engage in a meaningful conversation with someone you are either negotiating or you are setting the stage for future negotiations.

According to the dictionary *negotiate* is defined as "to confer or discuss with another or others in order to come to terms or reach an agreement." The key phrases are "confer or discuss" and "reach an agreement." But, prior to you conferring or discussing, you need to determine what it is you want to reach agreement on.

Martti Ahtisaari, the former president of Finland, who earned a Nobel Peace Prize in 2008 for his serial successes in helping to defuse several of the world's thorniest conflicts, was awarded The Great Negotiator Award at Harvard University in September 2010.

During his acceptance speech Ahtisaari told an audience of faculty and students that at the outset of each negotiation, he stated clearly to all sides what he expected the outcome to be, and then gave the parties wide scope to reach that outcome.

Ahtisaari further stated that the key to any successful negotiation is knowing what outcome you want, and then figuring out how to get there.

I can readily attest that knowing the outcome you are trying to achieve is imperative to any successful negotiation. Once I was driving in the car with my wife and she was providing directions. As we were approaching a fork in the road I asked which way we should go and she responded "there," not indicating any direction in particular. While it was crystal clear to my wife which road I should take, it was not as evident to me, and consequently I ended up going the wrong way. Just like not being clear with giving or taking directions can result in your making the wrong turns, not being clear in what you are trying to achieve in a negotiation will result in an outcome you did not intend.

Many people reading this book are in the process of attempting to institute a major change in their lives. Perhaps you are trying to make more money, initiate a new chapter in your career, or start up a business venture. Or maybe you have the aspiration to accomplish bigger and better things, so you can create a difference in someone else's life.

Regardless of what you are attempting to accomplish, I am going to share with you five strategic questions you need to address, and provide some self-help assignments that will assist you in successfully negotiating to obtain whatever it is that you desire.

First Question:

What are your goals and objectives, or, said another way, through your negotiations or discussions, what are you trying to reach agreement on?

The key to any successful negotiation is being very clear on what outcome you are attempting to achieve.

I cannot begin to recite the number of times I have asked a person what their career aspiration is and they respond, "I want to be promoted." When they reply with that expression I normally follow up with, "If the organization you are working for promoted you today, that would accomplish your goal and make you happy?" Typically, they reply, "Yes, if I got promoted I would be very happy."

In this particular example if the person got promoted to, let me be absurd and say "chief gastronomical hygiene technician," otherwise known as a dishwasher, they would have achieved their objective.

Now, some people might say, "At least it is a promotion." The majority, however, would sarcastically respond, "You know what they meant, and that is definitely not the role they wanted to be promoted into."

The truth is if there is any confusion, or you are ambiguous regarding what your goals and objectives are, other people may think they have satisfied your desires, when in fact where you ended up was not remotely close to what you were attempting to achieve.

Above everything else, before you begin to negotiate with someone you have to crystallize what you are ultimately striving to accomplish.

Another way of answering the question I posed above regarding what your career aspiration is might be, "I want to be promoted into a position where I can make a significant contribution to the organization, while I continue to have opportunities to develop my skills, make more money, and advance in my career."

Although that may not completely encompass everything you want to achieve, it is at a minimum much more comprehensive, and you now have the basis for a meaningful conversation. Before you start to negotiate with someone it is imperative that you think through, write down, and clearly articulate what you want to accomplish.

It does not matter what your long-term goals or objectives are; you should always be strategizing around what you want to achieve, and the actions you need to be taking or putting in place, to provide you with the best chance to prevail in your negotiations.

This first self-help assignment highlights what you need to excogitate, and act upon, prior to entering into any negotiation.

Assignment #1:

Write down what specific outcomes you want to derive from your negotiation. Things you might want to consider include:

- Are your objectives abundantly clear, and are you conveying them in a manner that is easy for others to understand?

- Can you accomplish everything you want at one time, or will you need to separate your bigger goals into smaller objectives?

- If you attain what you are asking for today, how will it position you for the accomplishment of your long-term personal plan?

- How do the outcomes you are seeking conflict or align with the objectives of the person(s) you will be negotiating with?

- Is the person(s) you are going to be negotiating with the one that will make the ultimate decision?

- Are you prepared – mentally, financially – for what may result from the negotiation?

Second Question:

What are you willing to do, or relinquish, to obtain what you are seeking?

Some people, once they have figured out what they want to accomplish during the negotiation, stop there and think their task is complete. Unfortunately, figuring out the desired objectives that you want to derive from the negotiation is just the beginning.

Once you have a clear understanding of what you want to extract from the negotiation, the next hurdle is to ascertain how far you are willing to go, and how much you are willing to sacrifice, to realize your objectives.

It is fairly easy to articulate what you want to achieve. It is a lot more complicated to ascertain what it will take to achieve your objectives. And more importantly, you have to determine if you are willing to devote the time, and endure the consequences, required to obtain the outcomes you desire. Therein lies the dilemma.

Reverting back to my earlier example, after communicating to me that they want to be promoted, I follow up with questions such as:

- Are you qualified for the role you want to ascend to?

- Would you be willing to relocate and take a developmental assignment in another city, or faraway country, to achieve the promotion?

- How important is spending quality time with your family?

- Are you willing to put in an additional twenty to thirty hours a week to learn the new role and demonstrate your level of commitment?

- Would you take educational or language classes at night to further enhance your skills?

What I counsel people to do is, deal with the facts, not your emotions, and in the process, be completely honest with yourself. Are the sacrifices you are going to be required to make, to obtain what you want, really worth it to you?

If what you are seeking does not merit your complete undivided attention, or you are not totally dedicated to doing whatever it takes to be successful in your negotiation, you may need to revise your plan. As I mentioned in an earlier chapter, doing something you are not comfortable with to get something you think you want will cause you failure, heartache, and pain.

I have heard people when they are in the midst of a negotiation say, "I will do whatever it takes," but in their heart they knew it was not a true statement. Ultimately a situation inevitably arises that requires them to do something they have known from the very beginning would be an issue. And, they either renege on the commitment they made during the negotiation, or attempt to renegotiate. Neither of these is a good situation to be in and could have negative implications on the accomplishment of your long-term plans.

It does not matter what you are attempting to accomplish via your negotiation, to be better than your best you have to be honest with yourself and one hundred percent committed to winning all of the time. If you know in your heart that you cannot be totally dedicated to effectuating what you are pursuing, then it is best to select a different path, or wait for a more suitable opportunity before you attempt to proceed.

Far too often people only focus on the positives, and neglect to take into account the challenges required to obtain their goals. Therefore, before you begin to negotiate make sure you really and truly understand the implications of what you are asking for, and what commitment, or sacrifice, it will take to achieve the outcomes you desire.

Assignment #2:

- Write down the *specific* tasks you will need to execute to successfully accomplish the goal(s) you outlined in assignment #1. Questions to consider include:

- Why are you the best person for this opportunity, or more specifically, what problem will you solve, and why should anyone be willing to assist you in achieving your objective?

- What will be your biggest challenges if you are going to be successful in achieving the outcomes you desire?

- Do you require additional skills, training, or resources to accomplish the objectives you are negotiating for?

- Are you honest and truly willing to devote the extra time, energy, and effort required for you to be successful?

- Would you relocate, or travel extensively if necessary, to obtain what you are seeking?

- Do you have any family or personal restrictions that might inhibit your ability to be successful?

- Are you willing to forego the minor things you *want*, so you can focus on acquiring the major things you *need* to accomplish your long-term objectives?

- Are you adequately prepared to deal with any financial or emotional hurdles you may encounter?

Third Question:

What are you bringing to the table, or said another way, what experience, knowledge, skill set, or resources do you have to offer the other person you are negotiating with?

Most people do not see themselves as being a salesperson, but the truth is you are constantly in the business of selling yourself. Each and every day you are showcasing and marketing your current skills, expertise, talents, future potential, and value-adding abilities.

Do not underestimate the fact that everything you have done, and everything people think you can do, will be taken into consideration when you are attempting to come to terms or reach an agreement with someone.

I advise people that prior to entering into a negotiation, you need to eliminate the potential barriers that could inhibit you from not obtaining what you are seeking.

If you need to demonstrate you are an effective leader, take on a special project, or participate in a course, that will enhance your leadership skills. If you want to be more strategic, spend additional time refining your understanding of the organization's key initiatives and competitors. If improving your public speaking is a necessity, join a Toastmasters group. And, I could go on and on. The bottom line is, you have to be acutely aware of your strengths and weaknesses, and be able to articulate why what you have to offer is important to the person you are negotiating with.

It is imperative that you understand what is important to the person you are negotiating with, because what is significant to him or her should also be important to you. Knowing what motivates the person you are in discussions with, and understanding what they value, can prove beneficial and assist you in achieving your objectives.

Remember that you are marketing yourself every day, and your sales pitch starts well before you begin the official negotiation. Therefore, be proactive and do not provide people a reason not to invest in you and support what you are attempting to accomplish.

Assignment #3:

Write down what benefits you can provide the other person you are negotiating with. Also, highlight why they should be willing to assist you, or endow you with what you are seeking. Things to consider include:

- How will the person(s) you are negotiating with benefit from rendering you what you want?

- What differentiates you from other people who might be campaigning for the same outcome you desire? And, what value, expertise, or advantage will you contribute that others do not possess?

- What problems are you going to solve, and how will supporting you over someone else make things substantially better for the other person?

Fourth Question:

Are you inclined to "play the game" and endure complex situations, or arduous people, to obtain what you want?

People are oftentimes frustrated by what they consider to be unfair treatment. On many occasions, especially when something does not go their way, people have said to me, "That is not fair."

You know what? I wholeheartedly agree that there are times when things in life are not completely fair. Now that you understand situations and circumstances are not always unbiased, what are you going to do? Are you going to let someone, or something, prevent you from reaching your long-term goals?

You cannot spend your precious time trying to make rational something or someone who is irrational. You also should not expect that a situation will always be fair, or assume other people will uncondition-ally help you or be happy for your success.

The fact is there are a lot of miserable people in this world who consider it their personal mission to make things difficult for you. If you have not come across one of these people, consider yourself fortunate, but also know that sooner or later you may unfortunately encounter one of these tortuous individuals.

Whether it is an undesirable boss, an incompetent coach, or an en-vious colleague, the secret is to ascertain the best way to limit your exposure to people like this, and in the process not allow these indi-viduals to penetrate and destroy your dreams. At the same time you have to maintain a strong conviction or believe in yourself, and ad-here to the principles detailed in this book to help you achieve your objectives.

Some of you will still say, "It is not right. If I have to 'play the game' to achieve what I want, then I would rather not participate." My re-sponse to that is always be true to yourself and never compromise your personal values. On the other hand, you also need to be cog-nizant of the fact that just because you think things are not fair, it does not mean everyone else sees it the same way. Other people may unfortunately agree with the person who is blocking your path to suc-cess, and your reactions could directly influence whether or not you achieve your stated objectives.

Learning how to navigate difficult situations, and difficult people, while staying true to yourself, can be extremely frustrating, but you need to have faith, stay positive, and maintain focus on the satisfac-tion you will derive from accomplishing your long-term goals.

It will not be easy, but ultimately you will prevail if you believe in yourself and execute the strategies we have discussed in this and prior chapters.

Assignment #4:

Write down the relationships and actions you can pursue that can assist you in dealing with the difficult people, and formidable situations, you will encounter during your negotiations. Things to consider include:

- Do you know people who are currently, or were previously, successful in navigating around this difficult situation or person?

- What connections do you have that can be advantageous to you, and leveraged, as you attempt to work through this challenging situation?

- How can things you have accomplished previously serve as an example of your abilities, and positively reflect on what you are capable of achieving?

- Can one or more of your mentors be a resource, or reference, for helping you deal with this situation?

- What actions should you take to ensure conflicting personalities do not become an obstacle in the pursuit of your success?

- How can you ensure the appropriate decision makers are involved in the negotiations? And, what tactics can you take that will heighten your bargaining position?

Fifth Question:

What can and should you be proactively doing today to elevate your probability for success tomorrow?

Every time I enter into a negotiation, I expect to have a favorable outcome and achieve my objectives. The reason my expectations revolve around my being successful is because I make certain I am well prepared before I initiate the negotiation. I know what I want to accomplish, and I understand what it is going to take to achieve my objectives. I am aware of the obstacles that stand in my path, and I believe I will prevail against all odds.

Negotiations are an evolving process. Therefore, you should be preparing today, right now, for what you want to achieve in the future. Do not provide people a reason to say you are not qualified for, or capable of, achieving the goals you have outlined for yourself.

Remember you only lose if you are not prepared, give up, or are forced to quit. Do not let situations or people prevent you from being better than your best.

Above everything else you have to maintain focus on what you are trying to achieve. Do not take everything personally, make excuses, or let a setback, an unpleasant relationship, or a disastrous experience prevent you from obtaining what you deserve.

Be mindful of what you are attempting to accomplish, and stick to your plan, because if you become emotional or your perspective becomes clouded, you may very well miss a tremendous opportunity.

When it comes to negotiating to obtain what you want, winning is not the primary objective; winning is the only objective.

Assignment #5:

Write down what you need to change, or begin doing, to enhance your negotiating position. Things to consider include:

- Will getting an advanced degree, or taking a specific training course, place you in a better position to derive what you are asking for or attempting to achieve?

- How can you expand your network to interact more frequently with people who can be advantageous in helping you achieve your goals and objectives?

- What can you do to demonstrate your grasp of a particular skill set or expertise?

- What is the person you will be negotiating with interested in, and how can you convince him or her that you are the best solution to help him or her achieve what is important to them?

- How can you anticipate potential issues, and eliminate reasons for the other person not supporting the outcome you are seeking?

Let me leave you with a couple of final points related to negotiating that every good negotiator adheres to.

The specific aim in any negotiation is to shift the odds in your favor, thereby enhancing the probability that you will be victorious. With that in mind, you should have a list of non-negotiable items that include the things you definitively must receive, as well as actions or demands that you absolutely need to avoid accepting. Along with the points you will not compromise on, you need to know when it is to your advantage to walk away from the negotiation. If discussions during the negotiation begin to go against your personal plan, moral values, or ultimate goals, you need to walk away and reassess the situation. Every good negotiator has non-negotiable items and a walk-away point. Without these there are no boundaries to your negotiations and you will fail, or end up with an unsatisfactory conclusion that will keep you from what you are ultimately attempting to accomplish.

Another important piece of advice is to never underestimate the power of silence. Many people feel as if during a negotiation they have to do all of the talking. Asking questions and listening more than you speak provides perspective, demonstrates maturity, and can very often be beneficial in a negotiation.

Also, if you are planning to negotiate with the person again, do not make them feel like they lost or they will never be open to assisting you again. If at all possible avoid backing the other person into a corner. Leave them options that encourage their support for what you are trying to achieve, while allowing them to maintain their dignity and respect.

Finally, when you enter into a negotiation do not memorize a speech, or ad-lib your message. Condense what you want to say into salient points and prepare a fluid, unscripted communication. Being familiar and comfortable with what you want to say will help you be less anxious, and further enhance your odds of obtaining what you want.

While being successful in a negotiation is not easy, I firmly believe that by following the guidelines outlined in this chapter and completing the self-help assignments, you will be well prepared to accomplish your objectives.

Pursue your destiny with the determination and belief that you can, and will, be successful. "Negotiate to Get What You Want," but also remember all of the people who support you along the way, because "It Is Not Just About You."

It Is Not Just About You

Being respected is far more conducive to your success than being liked or feared…

I was watching a movie once where a reputed mobster asks an adversary just before he was about to snuff him out if it was better to be feared or liked. If you were in the mobster's world, it definitely was advantageous to be feared. In spite of that I have observed in your pursuit of success it is far better to be respected than be feared or merely liked. Fear has a negative connotation, which can sway people to avoid contact, or interaction, with you. And, while being liked can be important, being respected is a more valuable asset. Along with helping to make you a better person, being respected and held in high esteem could play a significant role in facilitating your success.

Many self-help books are singularly focused on the merits of promoting or improving yourself, and engage very little, if at all, on the prospect of assisting yourself by contributing to the furtherance of others.

In this chapter I expound on the concept that each and every one of us has a talent, gift, or service we can extend to other people. And, although it should not be your sole reason for giving back, doing something that benefits others can make you feel virtuous, knowing you have made a positive impact on someone else's life.

My grandmother "Mazzie" was the kindest-hearted person I have ever known. Not only did she go out of her way to spoil all of her grandchildren, which she felt was her God-given right as a grandmother, she also would invite anyone, and I emphasis "anyone," she met who did not have a place to go to her home for Thanksgiving dinner.

Growing up I fondly remember the diverse array of people who joined our family at Grandmother's house for Thanksgiving dinner over the years. And you can only imagine not all of them were reputable characters. However, despite what others in the family might have thought, my grandmother could not be persuaded to discontinue encouraging complete strangers to partake in our annual gathering.

The motto my grandmother lived her life by was founded on the verse in Luke 12:48, "For everyone to whom much is given, of him/her shall much be required."

My grandmother's continuous quoting of this passage from Luke's gospel always rang true to me in my youth. But, as a teenager it resonated even more with me, especially when I learned that this passage was the same one that Rose Kennedy constantly instilled into her children to encourage their service to help others. There was a time when Rose Kennedy's husband, Joseph P. Kennedy, was cited as being the richest man in America. To say that my grandmother was not rich or on the Forbes list of the richest Americans is an understatement. What is striking however in this comparison is that the term "to whom much is given, much shall be required" does not just mean money. It means so much more. It can mean providing moral support, encouraging, advising, or praying for someone. Every person, regardless of their status or position in life, has the opportunity, and the obligation, to make a difference in the lives of others.

I would like to believe that some of my grandmother's passion for helping others, without the expectations of receiving anything in return, rubbed off on me. That certainly could be questioned, since I admittedly have not maintained my grandmother's tradition of inviting complete strangers to my home for Thanksgiving dinner.

Nevertheless, I will confess to being a person who believes it is a privilege to be in a position where I can provide advice and make an impact in someone's life. I am also a staunch advocate of persuading others to be better than their best.

Whether we care to acknowledge it or not, most of us are egotistical and self-centered. And heretofore, throughout the various chapters in this book, I have primarily concentrated on the assorted activities you should do to aggrandize yourself.

While taking personal responsibility for your own success and happiness is definitely important, I also want to encourage you to take every opportunity to mentor, support, and be a role-model for others in the same manner that you want, and need, people to assist you in your endeavors.

Being better than your best requires that you become a better man/woman, husband/wife, father/mother, and friend/colleague. So as you strive to achieve your own personal success, make sure you take the time to extend a hand down to help lift others up.

A couple of my good personal friends, who exemplify the motto "It Is Not Just About You," are Nancy and Matt McKenna.

After a successful career at PepsiCo Matt retired and joined Keep America Beautiful, Inc., as president and CEO, to pursue his true passion of making a difference and giving back to the community. "There is so much power in bringing volunteers to community improvement," says Matt. "Recycling, community gardens, and litter prevention are tools for local and neighborhood environmental change. We are clearly seeing evidence that the longer a community focuses on anti-litter education programs, the more successful their efforts will be."

Matt goes on to say, "Non-profit organizations need the same operating disciplines that exist in public companies. I have been fortunate to carry over the experiences I learned at PepsiCo to Keep America Beautiful."

Equally impressive is the work that Nancy does with the Mount Vernon, New York, senior high school "championship" basketball team. Matt and Nancy do not reside in Mount Vernon, but over the years Nancy had helped numerous players from the basketball team prepare for and get accepted into college. For many of these young men they are the first in their families to attend college, so Nancy's efforts are, to say the least, life changing.

Both Matt and Nancy are successful law school graduates, and could rightfully be spending their time, energy, and money just on themselves and their own four children. But instead, they embrace the satisfaction that comes from helping others achieve their goals of living a successful and happy life.

The efforts put forth by Nancy and Matt could be considered an anomaly or exception. But thankfully, it is not. Everyday people from all walks of life are going out of their way to assist others. You too have a tremendous opportunity to help others, and in the process have a positive impact on the world around you.

A reciprocal benefit of lending yourself to helping others is that in the process you are enriched and empowered. Giving back, and not expecting anything in return for your support and assistance, is truly the greatest reward that comes from assisting others.

Therefore, when you are vigorously pursuing success and happiness, I want to encourage you to refrain from being solely focused on advancing your own ambitions at the expense of others. Invest some of your time, energy, and resources into meaningful circumstances that have a positive impact on other people, and society as a whole.

As you grow, develop, and achieve your goals, one of the many ways you can express "It Is Not Just About You" is to pass along what you have learned to other bright and talented family members, friends, and colleagues so they too can benefit from your experiences.

You have a responsibility, and an obligation, to those coming behind you to provide them with the value of your insights, so they can profit from your guidance and avoid some of the pitfalls and mistakes you encountered.

One of the greatest satisfactions of a true leader comes from seeing people they have mentored and counseled be successful. Achieving success and happiness will be hollow and empty if you make it all about you. To be meaningful it also has to be about giving back and creating opportunities for others.

A significant component of the reward you receive from assisting others comes from knowing someone else is happier, or in a better position to fulfill their dreams and aspirations, as a result of you. Therefore, as you strive to achieve your goals and objectives, take every opportunity to be a mentor and share the experiences and insights you have acquired along the way.

Now before we go any further, I want to emphatically state for the record that while I believe you must be willing to assist others, you cannot, and should not, take responsibility for "fixing" someone else. And, quite frankly, as much as you may want to or how hard you try, you cannot help everybody; nor should you.

The fact of the matter is, some people have an entitlement mentality and believe things are owed to them, or you should do for them, without their having to put forth any effort to earn it.

It is imperative to keep this in perspective, because there are people who have reached out to help and mentor others only to have those individuals not show the willingness to put forth any effort to help themselves. As a result the situation only got worse.

An example of this is a man named Robert who graduated from college with a master's degree in educational counseling. After graduation Robert accepted a position in a private school for troubled youth, working as both a teacher and director for one of the school's dorm houses. Despite Robert's commitment and best efforts, the group of adolescents in his dorm ended up not making progress in school, and some proceeded to get involved with drugs and other criminal acts. The fact that the kids spiraled into disaster was primarily their own doing, and in no way due to lack of effort, concern, or dedication on Robert's part.

Unfortunately, this episode haunted Robert for the rest of his life. Considering himself a failure and unfit to lead others, Robert left the school and went to work as a crew member on fishing and lobster boats, which he was still doing some 35 years later.

The lesson to be derived from Robert's experience is you cannot help everyone, should not take someone else's failure personally, and are not solely responsible for what happens to others.

Along with people who are unwilling to put forth any effort to assist themselves, there are also individuals who would rather spend time dwelling on the misery they are in. These individuals do not really and truly want to be helped, and would rather complain about their situation, as opposed to working on changing their situation.

So when your support is requested, you need to fully assess whether it is really beneficial to invest your precious time and resources trying to assist someone who does not have the will, or desire, to change and help themselves.

Ultimately you have to ensure the people you are attempting to help want and appreciate your support, because if they are not truly committed and willing to partner with you, they can impede your success and pull you down with them.

Everyone has heard stories of a person who tried to save someone that was drowning. The person who was drowning was so scared and focused on their current situation that instead of relaxing, and gently holding onto the person that was attempting to save them, they panicked. And in their fight for survival the person who needed to be saved frantically pulled their potential savior under the water, and they both eventually drowned.

When you are attempting to assist someone, remember that the only person completely responsible for your personal success, or failure, is you. And, while it is not all about you, before you can add value to anyone else you have to first be in a position to change and help yourself.

The following quote illustrates why you first need to change yourself in order to be in a position to help others:

"When I was a young man, I wanted to change the world. I found it was difficult to change the world, so I tried to change my nation. When I found I could not change the nation, I began to focus on my town. I could not change the town and as an older man, I tried to change my family. Now, as an old man, I realize the only thing I can change is myself, and suddenly I realize that if long ago I had changed myself, I could have made an impact on my family. My family and I could have made an impact on our town. Their impact could have changed the nation and I could indeed have changed the world." — Author Unknown

At the end of the day you need to have a social conscience, and live your life so the people around you feel important and valued. Then they in turn can make the people around them feel important and valued, creating a positive circle of life.

Doing something for someone else without expecting anything in return is but one of the numerous attributes of service. Many ordinary things that you do can have a profound effect on other people. For example, engaging in simple tasks such as encouraging a coworker or teammate, participating in a charity event, introducing a friend to someone they do not know, listening sincerely, or openly praising a person in front of their boss or loved ones, are just a few of the ways you can demonstrate to others that it is not just about you. And in the process, it can have a monumental impact on their lives.

While doing research for this book, I spoke to so many people who were struggling with the concept of work/life balance. Specifically, they were confronted with the dilemma of balancing their career, personal relationships, and other responsibilities while still retaining time for themselves, let alone being able to fit in time to assist others. While the subject of work/life balance could be the topic of its own book, it suffices to say that when it comes to adeptly managing a career, family, and personal time, maintaining work/life balance is difficult, if not impossible. The key is determining at what stages you need to shift focus, and flex your priorities, to keep your personal plan on track.

Before she had children my daughter enjoyed her job in the medical profession, traveled extensively across the United States, and volunteered her services at shelters and clinics. Then her first son was born and my daughter's priorities shifted, from being a person who was focused on all of the things that previously were important in her career and personal life, to being a mother.

As I have discovered over the years, the best mothers know that once their baby enters the world it is not just about them, it is about their children. And honestly, they would not have it any other way. Even on Mother's Day, great moms know it is not about them. In my daughter's case it is about celebrating the fact that she now has two precious sons in her life. Despite their occasional mischievous behavior, she would not trade her little guys for anything in the world — although at various times both of them have tested this theory.

When it comes to their family, successful people realize that being a parent of young children means there is limited balance in your life, you are no longer the center of attention, and you are in the business of taking care of little people who cannot yet take care of themselves. So no matter your marital or relationship status, when you are considering whether or not to purely focus on yourself, take a lesson from my daughter and realize at certain stages in your life, for various reasons, you have to flex your person plan and focus on the necessities of other people.

Noted British statesman and orator Sir Winston Churchill said it best: "We make a living by what we get, but we make a life by what we give."

Another important attribute of "It Is Not Just About You" is having the maturity to forgive someone. There are countless stories of people who have failed to achieve their ultimate goal because they could not let go of, and get over, the hurt and anger that someone had caused them. It is no coincidence that when you hear people talk about someone who could not put a situation behind him or her, it is always in the context of describing how that particular person failed to achieve something in their life.

Holding grudges, having animosity, or harboring bad feelings towards someone else will keep you anchored to your past, and prevent you from attaining all of the success that awaits you in your future. Before you can get better you have to first stop being bitter.

An event that sticks out in my mind about holding grudges concerns the news reports of the hundredth birthday of Joe Binder, a Bronx parking lot attendant who worked five days a week and had no plans to retire. In the TV news segments and newspaper articles, when he was asked what the secret to his longevity was, Joe gave only one standard answer, "Don't hold grudges."

Although your feelings might well be justified, you must realize that spending time, energy, and effort thinking about, or trying to get even, is detrimental. Until you forgive someone you are giving him or her control of your emotions, and you cannot move forward in a positive way.

I have known people who have spent a majority of their life being angry and upset about something that happened years ago. In fact, these people have held a grudge for so long that they have forgotten what caused them to be angry in the first place.

Regardless of the magnitude of your disagreements, forgiving some-one requires that although you may not literally forget, you do need to emotionally let go of the situation so that you and the other person can move forward with your respective lives.

Living a happy, purposeful, successful life requires that you come to the realization that "It Is Not Just About You." Always strive to leave the world, and each person you meet, in a better place, and as you seek to do so remember "Failure Is Not an Option."

CHAPTER Nine

Failure Is Not an Option

Everything you need to be successful is within your control. Start by looking deep within yourself…

Throughout this book I have focused on the fundamental attributes that are necessary for you to be better than your best. If taken seriously and applied appropriately, I am confident that the knowledge you have acquired thus far will be extremely beneficial as you pursue your dreams.

I want to pause for a moment, provide a different perspective, and share with you some of the traits that will cause you to derail, and not be successful, or achieve your personal goals.

Throughout my professional career and continuing to this day, I have devoted a substantial amount of time and energy, mentoring, and counseling people in all facets of their lives. Just as important as understanding what was required to accomplish their goals and objectives was being cognizant of what aspects of their current behavior were contributing to them falling short of their expectations.

There are a series of actions that will cause you to not actualize your dreams and aspirations. First among them is becoming too captivated by the negative aspect of the "what if" phenomenon.

Rather than focusing on the positives outcomes that can be derived from possessing desire, determination and dedication, far too often people become overly fixated with why they believe things will not turn out right for them. What if it does not work, what if they say no, what if he or she does not like me, what if I do not get the job, promotion, or contract, what if they cut me from the team, what if I lose? You can become so mentally constrained by all of the things that could possibly go wrong that you never stop to consider what if it all goes right.

Melissa Ann Lawson was the sixth winner of the television program *Nashville Star*, a country music singing competition seeking to find new country music artists. A mother with five children, she was the oldest competing contestant the year she won. After winning the competition she released her debut single "What If It All Goes Right," which she went on to sing at the 2008 Summer Olympics in Beijing, China.

The message conveyed in the song expresses what people who perpetually focus on the negative connotation of "what if" never seem to grasp. There is always a possibility that things may go wrong. Albeit with desire, determination, and dedication there is an even greater likelihood that things will turn out right and your dreams will be fulfilled.

Being fixated on the negative "what if" aspect of any situation will paralyze your ability to aggressively pursue your goals. Worst yet, it will prevent you from obtaining your rightfully deserved reward. You need to think positively, and expect superior results from all of your actions.

Consider the biblical story of David and Goliath. David, who was a young teenager, was able to slay Goliath, a gigantic man measuring over nine feet tall and possessing full military armor, including a sword, spear, and shield, by merely using a slingshot and a stone.

David had faith on his side and a solid plan of attack, so he was not focused on what if I miss or what if he kills me first. Armed with a simple slingshot, David was confident and did not stop to ponder not being successful. He knew the task that was in front of him and he responded accordingly. Finding a weakness in Goliath's armor David flew a stone into the giant's forehead, instantly bringing him down.

I am sure you have faced challenges in your life that were much more trivial than the giant David encountered. Yet you become so overwhelmed by the negative "what if" phenomenon that it paralyzes you, causing you not to achieve your goals and objectives.

I have encountered innumerable people who were afraid of achieving success because they were stagnated by the thought that other people would then expect more of them, and they were not confident they could meet the higher expectations.

A prime example is someone who does not apply for a higher position because they do not have sufficient confidence in their ability to be successful in a role they have trained, studied, worked hard, and are qualified for. As a result, they settle for less than they are capable of, and allocate a significant amount of their time and energy expounding on all of the reasons things probably would not have worked anyway, or why they could not be successful. To be better than your best you have to eradicate the "I cannot do something" attitude and develop an "I can do anything" attitude.

Alexander Haig is best remembered for being President Ronald Reagan's first Secretary of State. When he was growing up Haig wanted to attend West Point Military Academy and have a career in the

U.S. Army. As a high-school senior, Haig looked like a sure bet to get the coveted appointment to the famed academy. Yet Haig, his family, and his teachers were shocked when he did not receive an appointment to West Point. Most people would have been dismayed and abandoned such lofty dreams, but the disappointment only delayed Haig's dreams for a few minutes. Haig deferred going to college elsewhere, applied to the academy again the following year, and got admitted into West Point on his second try. Haig did not allow the negative thought of "what if" I try again and do not get admitted prevent him from pursuing his dream. Instead he went full force towards his lifelong goal of going to West Point. Needless to say, both Haig, who went on to have a distinguished career in the military, rising to the rank of four-star general, and West Point, made the appropriate decision.

Focusing only on the negative aspects of "what if" and not having confidence or faith in your own abilities, is a definite way to end up not being better than your best.

Another trait that will result in your failing to achieve all that you are capable of is not having big dreams, or being satisfied with average results. Almost everyone I know who has achieved great things had big dreams, which they turned into big goals with even bigger expectations. Big dreams invoke great confidence, which allows you to push yourself to even greater heights. And, while big dreams do not always culminate into monumental results, it is even more remote that small dreams, and minimal expectations, will end up producing a significant outcome.

One person who exemplifies the notion of having big dreams is Fred Smith, founder, president, and chief executive officer of Federal Express; the first worldwide overnight delivery service. The story goes that while attending college at Yale, Smith had to write a paper that was intended to be a business plan for a new start-up company. Smith wrote a detailed plan for an overnight delivery service in which packages would be collected and sent to a centralized hub in Memphis, Tennessee, and then distributed out to destinations across the country, and across the world. To say that Smith was disheartened when he received a C for this project is an understatement. After Yale, Smith served in the U.S. military as a Marine pilot in Vietnam, earning a Bronze Star, a Silver Star, and two Purple Hearts. Following his military service, Smith was convinced that his dream of an overnight delivery service was a winner, despite what his professor at Yale had thought. Using the same business plan, Smith was successful in attracting enough investors so he could start Federal Express. It is probably safe to assume that being persistent in following his dream was the best thing that Smith ever did in his professional life.

Now some of you may be thinking, "I do not want to be embarrassed, or disappointed, by having big dreams and big expectations, and then falling short." So instead of stretching beyond your comfort zone you lower your expectations, and settle for safe, moderate goals. I would respond to that behavior in two ways. First, you should never let the fear of failing deter you from pursuing big dreams. Second, there is no embarrassment in shooting for the moon and landing amongst the stars. Trying something and not reaching your original goal is not a failure. The failure is in not trying at all.

Whatever you attempt to accomplish in your life, you should aim as high as you possibly can. Put your heart and soul into achieving magnanimous goals, because even if you do not reach your original objectives you will still have done exceptionally well. And in either case, you would have exceeded what others thought was possible. Having big dreams, and believing that you can and will be successful, will set you apart from others, and offers the best chance for you to be better than your best.

My oldest son played basketball at Bowdoin College, which is located in Brunswick, Maine. During his sophomore year the basketball team won thirteen of their games and lost twelve. Entering my son's junior year one of the team's goals was to win more games than they had the previous year. Halfway through the schedule his team had won eleven of their first thirteen games, well on their way to a great season.

Over the balance of the season the basketball team only won three of their final ten games, to finish with fourteen wins and ten losses. Did the Bowdoin basketball team achieve their objective? In terms of winning one more game than the previous year, "yes" they did. The real question, however, is did they dream big enough and achieve all they were capable of?

You could arguably attribute the collapse in the second half of the basketball season to pathetic coaching, poor playing, a tougher schedule, or a combination of all of the above. However, when you delve a little deeper what you would also discover is my son's basketball team was capable of doing better, but the team set their ambitions too low, did not dream big enough, had minimal expectations, and became satisfied with a goal that felt comfortable and did not require much risk. As a result the Bowdoin men's basketball team has ended up being perennial underachievers.

You have to always dream big, have even bigger expectations, and believe in your heart that you will be successful. You also cannot make excuses, or be afraid, or unwilling to reach beyond what may seem possible, because it will result in your not reaching your full potential. And, by the way, just because you have not been successful in the past does not mean that you cannot change your future.

Another factor that culminates in people not achieving their goals is being afraid to make a mistake. In fact, the biggest mistake you can make is being afraid of making a mistake. Wayne Gretzky, who was a famous hockey player, is associated with the saying, "You miss 100% of the shots you do not take." While that is true in sports it is also true in life.

Successful people understand that to achieve their goals, they cannot be afraid to make mistakes. Mistakes are part of the process of learning and realizing your goals and objectives. If you do not make any mistakes, chances are you are not pushing yourself to be better than your best.

This is not to suggest you have to make all of the mistakes yourself. You can also gain valuable insights and learn from others who have made mistakes, thereby preventing you from having to repeat their misfortunes.

One of the contributing factors in people being afraid to make mistakes is that throughout your life, at home, in school, or in the work place, you are frequently warned against making mistakes. People condition you to believe that as long as you are mindful, do tasks slowly and carefully, and learn from the errors of others, there is no need for you to make a mistake.

Therefore, when you do make a mistake you fear being criticized for not being diligent enough, not thinking things through, or not listening. As a result of what you have been constantly told you become afraid of making even the smallest mistake, and in the process let other people define for you what you are capable of achieving.

Baseball Hall of Famer Ted Williams holds the major-league baseball record for the highest batting average over a complete season. Yet despite his record .406 average, the man who some proclaim to be the greatest baseball hitter who ever lived only got a hit in approximately four out of every ten batting attempts during his record-setting year. The truth is no matter how talented you are, no one has a perfect batting average, or competes at a high level in any aspect of their life, without making a mistake.

No matter how smart or talented a person may be, no one is perfect. That is an impossible task, and to always strive for perfection, with the fear of never making a mistake, is an unquestionable way to guarantee failure. Also, all of the time, energy, and effort you put into trying to avoid making mistakes limits your growth, and discourages you from trying new and different things.

To be better than your best, you have to reprogram yourself to accept the fact that a mistake is not a failure. A mistake is merely a learning opportunity and a stepping-stone on your path to success.

Holding back until all of the conditions for success are perfect, or hoping things will magically change in your favor before you decide to move forward, is another attribute that will cause you to subvert or not reach your full potential.

Although having patience may be a virtue, indecisiveness and being complacent is not. Waiting for a catalyst before making a change could very well cause you to miss a great opportunity.

If you constantly delay putting plans into action until the right time, right circumstances, or right person comes into your life, or continue to do the same thing and expect to get a different result, it will only postpone, or potentially eliminate, your chance for success. Unfortunately, most people need to reach a desperate place in their lives before they are motivated to make a change. For some, losing a job or business deal might do it. For others it is a change in a relationship or their family situation.

The point is if you become paranoid, or are waiting for the perfect opportunity before initiating a change, you will never be better than your best.

The famous humorist Will Rogers once said, "Even if you are on the right track you'll get run over if you just sit there." So do not spend so much time trying to choose the perfect opportunity that you miss the right opportunity.

Now I want to stress that I am not suggesting for one minute that you should just accept the first opportunity that comes your way. To the contrary, I am saying that you need to be prepared, and activate your plan early enough, so you can choose the "appropriate opportunity" when it comes along.

It is also important to remember, "Opportunities are never lost; someone will take the one you missed." —Author Unknown

Another aspect that can be critically detrimental to your achieving success is failing to continuously put forth extraordinary effort when pursuing your goals and objectives. Many people start out doing well, then become satisfied and comfortable with where they are and what they have accomplished. As a result, they do not continue to exert the dedication and motivation required to ultimately succeed.

I have also known people who became so frustrated with their current situation that they walked away and quit before the final outcome was decided. Your pursuit of success is never over until you have achieved your greatest dreams and aspirations. Successful people become so engrossed in, and fixated on, what they are trying to accomplish that they eat less, sleep less, and yes even play less. They understand that significant gain can come from a little pain, so they are willing to make short-term sacrifices to derive long-term benefits. And, no matter the circumstances, they never give up until their goals are accomplished.

I can still remember watching Super Bowl XXVII, when Dallas Cowboy player Leon Lett recovered a fumble and ran 64 yards downfield headed for the goal line and an all but certain touchdown. However, Lett started to celebrate prematurely and slowed down right before he reached the end zone. Before Lett crossed the goal line, a Buffalo Bills' player by the name of Don Beebe, who had been chasing Lett, slapped the ball out of his hands and Lett was denied the touchdown.

Lett's unfortunate blunder reinforces the fact that you can never become satisfied, stop putting forth the required effort, or prematurely begin to celebrate until you have completely accomplished your objective, which in Lett's case was scoring the touchdown.

I expressed in chapter one that most people want to win but hating to lose is more impactful. Therefore, you have to always put yourself in the best possible position to derive superlative results. Only by taking control of your destiny, dreaming big dreams, having viable options, staying positive, and constantly focusing on your long-term goals, can you expect to be better than your best.

As you ponder all of the things you need to begin doing to achieve your goals, also take the time to consider what you need to stop doing.

Remember, "Failure Is Not an Option," and in the process of contemplating your future ask yourself, "Are You in the Place You Are Supposed to Be?"

CHAPTER Ten

Are You in the Place You Are Supposed to Be?

If you do not know where you are going, any road will get you there…

One of the toughest challenges you will face in your life is determining what path you ought to take to derive the success you are seeking. Furthermore, how do you know whether you should be satisfied with what you have achieved, or if you should be striving for more?

What I have learned over the years is, success is not a destination. Success is a way of thinking and becomes an integral part of your life. Successful people appreciate and do not apologize for what they have accomplished. At the same time successful people also know they can always do more, reach new heights, and be a better person in the process.

Each and every day people all over the world are fulfilling their dreams, enhancing their careers, and embarking on happy, successful lives. You are just as competent, just as worthy, and just as talented as the next person. The only difference between where you are today, and being in the place you are supposed to be, is a methodical focus and determination that nothing, and no one, is going to prevent you from being better than your best.

Putting yourself in the best possible position to derive the maximum results, and living your life with no regrets, sounds like a cliché. Yet there is a lot of truth and merit to both of these statements.

If your desire is to be better than your best you cannot become satisfied, or complacent, with your current status and situation. Far too often people get comfortable, take the easy way out, and settle for where they are in life. As opposed to breaking the paradigm, expanding their comfort zone and striving to reach the goals that will put them where they should be in their life.

As I have stressed countless times throughout this book, having a written plan for your life is extremely important. But, unleashing the dedication required to activate your plan is paramount, and being singularly focused on pursuing whatever is required to complete your plan is epic.

The point is you will only be better than your best when you are in the appropriate place in your life, doing monolithic things with your life. Making excuses about why you cannot do, or achieve, something must become a thing of the past, and in its place you have to develop an excellence to eminence mentality.

I know a person with an advanced college degree who spent a couple of years working as a courier when he was going through a transitional phase in his career. One day he was driving down an interstate highway and saw a big billboard containing a verse from Romans 12:6 that read, "We all have different gifts, according to the grace given us, let us use them."

After reading that billboard, this person's life completely changed because in his heart he knew that working as a courier was not where he was supposed to be. His dream and passion was to do public relations work, which by the way he was extremely good at. Motivated by that scripture verse this individual changed his attitude, and seriously began to pursue opportunities that coincided with his dreams. Within a year he had relinquished his job as a courier and embarked on a successful career in public relations.

The excuses about why you cannot excel in your life, or navigate from the situation you are currently in to the place you are intended to be, hold no merit when you consider the powerful message on that billboard.

Over the past thirty years I have witnessed, time and time again, that successful people do not accept defeat, nor do they rest on their laurels. To be better than your best and achieve the success you are seeking, you must continuously exhibit the following traits.

Traits Required for Success:

- Take control of your future and activate the changes required to accomplish your dreams and aspirations.

- Hate to lose versus just playing to win. And, be dedicated to putting forth the extra effort necessary for you to succeed.

- Have a personalized vision of what you want to attain in your life, and what it is going to take to obtain it.

- Deal quickly and appropriately with a difficult situation, relationship, or challenge.

- Ask for help, and accept the fact that needing support and assistance is not a sign of weakness.

- Acknowledge that almost everyone you encounter will be smart and capable, in his or her own unique way, so you always need to be better than your best.

- Appreciate the importance of having integrity, and maintaining your moral compass.

- Understand how to develop and nurture a mentoring relationship so you can get honest feedback.

- Observe how organization politics could work to your advantage, and master the rules of the game.

- Be proactive in negotiating to derive benefits that will enhance your ability to achieve your objectives.

- Plan out your life and be willing to take calculated risks.

Not adhering to these traits, settling for less than you deserve, and failing to pursue the appropriate actions to put yourself in a better place or position, will keep you embroiled in a world of unhappiness and regret.

Achieving the goals you desire will take desire, determination, and dedication. And yes, you may have to consider other people, and other circumstances, in the process. However, you have to wake up each and every day invigorated with a purpose, and take meaningful steps, sometimes big, sometimes small, toward actualizing the life you desire.

The journey that is set before you and the challenges you will face are not new and unique. History is overflowing with examples of ordinary people who overcame significant obstacles to consummate exemplary things in their lives. These people were successful because they did not limit or confine their dreams and aspirations. They saw possibility where others only saw impossibilities. And, they dared to believe in themselves as opposed to letting fear, lack of resources, or the perception of others define for them what they were or were not capable of accomplishing.

While you should unequivocally enjoy the fruits of your labor, you can never become completely satisfied, or comfortable, with where you are in your life. Otherwise, you risk not getting to where you need to be or becoming the best you can be. People who have achieved outstanding results realized the place, and situation, they were in was not where they were intended to be. They had a higher calling and purpose in life. Hence, they took dramatic actions to change their circumstances.

Achieving success is a lot like ascending a ladder. When you are climbing always look up and focus on where you are going, and what you are attempting to achieve. Do not look down or look back, spending time on where you have been, or you will stumble and fall.

Just endeavoring to get by, and live a tolerable life, will not lead you to being better than your best. Therefore, I urge you, I challenge you, and I encourage you to start, right now this very minute, making the necessary changes in your life that will put you on the path to being in the place you are supposed to be.

You have it within yourself to fulfill your dreams and accomplish all of your goals and aspirations. How do I know? Because by investing your time to read this book, you have shown the initiative to take the first step toward being better than your best.

I started out as a meek, naïve, financially deprived kid from Columbus, Ohio, and years later ended up with a life, and family, that is significantly better personally, spiritually, and financially.

The road I traveled was not always easy, but the tradeoffs and sacrifices I made were worth it to my family and me. Along the way I discovered that everyone's dreams, aspirations, and purpose in life are different. You have to travel your own path to success and happiness. You cannot walk in another person's footsteps, and they in turn cannot walk in yours. Therefore, constantly comparing your journey to someone else's and wondering where they are in life, what material things they have accumulated, or how their career is progressing, will only cause you to lose focus on your own goals and objectives. You can only compare *your* stages of success to *your* own past successes or failures.

I fully understand and appreciate that it is human nature to compete and want to do better than the next person. However, as you develop your personal plan and begin to work toward your goals and objectives, always remember that the race is not always won by the swiftest, or the smartest.

Studies have shown that fifty percent of the population has an average intelligence quotient (IQ), while twenty-five percent process an above average IQ, and the other twenty-five percent a below average IQ. Since most people are equipped with an average IQ, the odds of someone being successful merely because they are smarter than you are not impossible, but it is very remote.

I cannot emphasize enough the importance of running your own race, having undeniable confidence in your abilities, and despite the seemingly insurmountable odds, sticking to your personal plan.

There will undoubtedly be times when you may question whether or not putting forth the effort to overcome the obstacles placed in your path is worth it. I want to ensure you that if your personal plan is well thought out, you have adeptly considered the pros and cons, and you are willing to invest the time, energy, and extra effort required to accomplish your goals, you will ultimately be successful. You are a winner, and part of winning is being successful despite the obstacles placed in your life. Therefore, never give up on yourself, no matter how distressing things may appear to be.

Whenever I begin to have doubts and get discouraged, I am reminded of the following story that my younger brother shared with me.

The only survivor of a shipwreck was washed up on a small, uninhabited island. Every day he scanned the horizon for help, but none seemed forthcoming. Exhausted, he eventually managed to build a little hut out of driftwood to protect him from the elements and store his few possessions. On day twenty, after scavenging for food, he arrived home to find his little hut in flames, with smoke rolling up to the sky. He felt the worst had happened, and everything was lost. He was stunned with disbelief, grief, and anger. Early the next day, he was awakened by the sound of a ship approaching the island that had come to rescue him. "How did you know I was here?" asked the weary man of his rescuers. "We saw your smoke signal," they replied.

It is human nature to get discouraged when things appear to be going bad, but you should never lose faith, because when your life seems to be going up in flames it just may be a smoke signal that summons the support and assistance you need.

In addition to all of the other wisdom and knowledge that I have shared with you throughout this book, I would advise you not to live a life that is full of regrets. Having repentance, or being despondent over something that has already occurred, and lamenting, after the fact, about how it could or should have been different, will cause you nothing but anguish. The time to act is when you can make a positive impact, not when the opportunity has eluded you. You have to capitalize on the moment and create your own success story.

The world will present you with more opportunities, good and bad, than you can possibly conceive. Your challenge is determining which goals you will seek, and how passionate you are going to be in pursuit of your dreams.

Although reading about success, talking about success, and observing how others achieve success are all noble attributes, these acts will serve no great purpose unless you use them as motivation to institute and implement your own personal plan for success.

Everyone is searching for the secret to success. So I will let you in on a little secret. The secret to success is, there is no secret. Success will not come to you, or happen for you — you have to go after it.

Success requires sacrifice, so you must have an unwavering focus on your goals and what you are trying to accomplish. In doing so your mental concentration, and dedication to your personal plan, needs to replicate that of a racehorse who wears blinders so they can only see straight ahead and not be distracted by what is going on around them. Likewise, you need to be singularly focused and give your utmost attention to the goals you are seeking to accomplish.

In your pursuit of success nothing can replace desire, determination, and unequivocal dedication. And, along with a relentless adherence to these three attributes, you have to chase your dreams as if your entire life depends on it.

I firmly believe you can obtain everything you desire as long as you put forth the required effort and commitment. No one ever said being successful was going to be easy. However, I can assure you that if you obtain something that, in your heart, you really and truly desire, it is worth it.

Successful people come from all walks of life, and their anecdotes of success abound. Let their experiences and their karma help fuel your own personal drive to succeed.

I once read this inspirational story, which might help to put what I am saying in perspective.

A business executive was deep in debt and could see no way out. Creditors were closing in on him. Suppliers were demanding payment. He sat on a park bench, head in hands, wondering if anything could save his company from bankruptcy. Suddenly an old man appeared before him. "I can see that something is troubling you," he said. After listening to the executive's woes, the old man said, "I believe I can help you." He asked the man his name, wrote out a check, and pushed it into his hand, saying, "Take this money. Meet me here exactly one year from today, and you can pay me back at that time." Then he turned and disappeared as quickly as he had come.

The business executive saw in his hand a check for $500,000, signed by John D. Rockefeller, then one of the richest men in the world! "I can erase my money worries in an instant!" he realized. But instead, the executive decided to put the check in his safe. Just knowing it was there might give him the strength to work out a way to save his business, he thought. With renewed optimism, he negotiated better deals and extended terms of payment. He closed several big sales. Within a few months, he was out of debt and making money once again.

Exactly one year later, he returned to the park with the check. At the agreed-upon time, the old man appeared. But just as the executive was about to hand back the check and share his success story, a nurse came running up and grabbed the old man. "I am so glad I caught him!" she cried. "I hope he has not been bothering you. He is always escaping from the rest home and telling people he is John D. Rockefeller." And, she led the old man away by the arm.

The astonished executive just stood there, stunned. All year long he had been wheeling and dealing, buying and selling, convinced he had half a million dollars in his safe that he could use if things did not go well. Suddenly, he realized that it was not the money, which in fact was not real, that had turned his life around. It was his newfound self-confidence that gave him the power to achieve anything he went after. —Author Unknown

With confidence you can go anywhere and accomplish anything you want. So have faith and believe in your abilities and yourself, because if you do not believe you can and will be successful, no one else will believe it either.

Life is about change, the choices you make, and the path you travel. The good news is, "it is all within your control." What you do, and how well you do it, will determine where you ultimately end up. Now is the time to start. This very minute! Quit procrastinating and commit to dramatically changing your life by putting into motion the wisdom and insights detailed in this book.

As you contemplate developing your personal plan, which outlines your dreams, goals, and aspirations, set your sights high, make every day count, and always expect to win. Above all else, remember where your true strength comes from. Build the life you have dreamed about, and then live it with all of your passion.

"You have brains in your head. You have feet in your shoes. You can steer yourself in any direction you choose. You're on your own. And you know what you know. You are the one who'll decide where to go." — Dr. Seuss

I sincerely hope reading this book was beneficial and will propel you to new heights, which culminates in great success. It is also my wish that this book will serve as a motivational guide, and be a valuable resource that you refer back to from time to time as you embark on your own personal journey to a successful and happy life.

I have the utmost confidence in you and your abilities and know that you will be immensely successful in achieving all of your wildest dreams, because "You Are Better Than Your Best."

CPSIA information can be obtained at www.ICGtesting.com
Printed in the USA
BVOW04s1832110315

391308BV00003B/154/P